THE **FONDUE** COOKBOOK

THE **FONDUE** COOKBOOK

BY GINA STEER

APPLE

A QUINTET BOOK

Published by Apple Press
Sheridan House
112-116A Western Road
Hove
East Sussex BN3 1DD

ISBN 1-84092-202-8

Reprinted 2000, 2001

This book was designed and produced by
Quintet Publishing Limited
6 Blundell Street
London N7 9BH

Creative Director: Richard Dewing
Art Director: Paula Marchant
Designer: Deep Design
Project Editor: Amanda Dixon
Editor: Margaret Gilbey
Photographer: Ian Garlick
Food Stylist: Kathryn Hawkins

Typeset in Great Britain by Central Southern Typesetters, Eastbourne
Manufactured in Singapore by Regent Publishing Services Limited
Printed in China by Leefung-Asco Printers Trading Limited

AUTHOR'S ACKNOWLEDGMENTS

**With thanks to Le Creuset for providing help and information relating to the history and tradition of the fondue.
Many thanks to my family and friends in the tasting of all the fondues.**

Some recipes in this book use raw eggs. Because of the slight risk of salmonella, raw eggs should not be served
to the very young, the ill or the elderly, or to pregnant women.

CONTENTS

INTRODUCTION

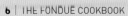

Fondues of all kinds are enjoyed throughout the world today. However, the dish originated many centuries ago in Switzerland as a result of the country's climate and geography, and fondue is now the Swiss national dish.

The harsh winters of the Alpine mountains meant small isolated villages could be cut off from the outside world for months at a time and food supplies were limited. The only readily available ingredients in many villages were cheese, wine and bread. As the winter dragged on, the cheese made in the summer began to dry out. The villagers needed to find a dish that would be both filling and sustaining but which also tasted good—hence the birth of fondue. The word *fondue* comes from the French word *fondre*, meaning to melt or to blend. The original Swiss fondue came from the region of Neuchâtel and was made with Gruyère and Emmentaler cheese. Other villages soon adopted the dish and created their own versions, using local cheese and produce.

Nowadays, we can find many varieties of fondue, and in this book I have featured a selection of my favourites. France is famous for its Fondue Bourguignonne (page 30), in which strips of prime steak are cooked in hot oil, then dipped into a savoury sauce. The Asian version (page 48) uses a Mongolian hot pot to cook the food in a fragrantly flavoured stock; other fondues consist of vegetables and meat dipped into a Japanese-style tempura batter and cooked in sizzling oil. Then there are deliciously wicked chocolate and fruit fondues for treats or dessert. As a matter of fact, almost any food can be cooked in a fondue pot, making it an easy and fun way to entertain your family and friends.

To keep a cheese fondue creamy, you must swirl the dippers in a figure of eight when dipping. Tradition has it that if you have the misfortune to lose your dipper in the fondue you have to pay a forfeit—a woman must kiss all the men present and a man must give the hostess either a bottle of wine or a glass of kirsch; if anyone loses their dipper again, they have to host the next fondue party.

While the fondue is sitting on the methylated spirit burner, a delicious crust is formed on the base of the pot. This is considered to be the greatest delicacy of the entire meal and should be shared equally among all the guests.

It is traditional not to drink cold drinks while eating, as it was always believed they would cause indigestion. Instead, unsweetened tea, warm fruit juice or even mulled wine would be served with the food, and a glass of cherry brandy, schnapps or kirschwasser would be offered in a 'rest period' halfway through the meal. However, a glass of the wine used in making the fondue would be an excellent accompaniment, preferably served at room temperature.

GUIDELINES

There is a variety of shapes and types of fondue pots available, even one designed especially for chocolate fondues. Whichever pot you have, there are a few guidelines to follow when using it.

- Before starting to use your fondue pot, read the manufacturer's instructions carefully and always take great care when transferring any hot oil or stock to the pot.
- Light the methylated spirit burner carefully and place on the table on a heatproof mat or surface. Never add extra fuel to the burner while it is lit or still hot.
- Do not used a damaged burner and when moving the hot fondue pot, handle with oven gloves or a thick cloth.
- Cheese and chocolate fondues burn easily and should be kept warm over a low heat.

CHEESE FONDUES

- When making a cheese fondue, use a heavy-based pan, metal-lined, with an enamel or a cast-iron base, or a heavy-glazed earthenware pot, as this will prevent the cheese from burning.
- Use strong-flavoured cheese: melt it slowly and once the fondue is transferred to the methylated spirits burner ensure it bubbles *gently*. Do not let it boil, or the cheese will become stringy. If this does happen, lower the heat and continue to cook gently until the cheese has melted and the mixture becomes smooth.
- Always choose a dry wine or cider, and do not worry if at first the cheese separates from the wine: just keep stirring and it will gradually become smooth and creamy.
- If the cheese forms a lump in the base of the pot, increase the heat slightly and keep stirring. If it curdles, add a teaspoonful of lemon juice and beat well; this should rescue your fondue.

- If the fondue becomes too thick, add a little extra warmed wine or cider; if it is too thin, add a little extra cornflour, blended with a little water.
- Bread for dipping should not be too fresh or it will crumble in the fondue. Salads should be offered as an accompaniment. If you realize your guests are still hungry (though fondues *are* very filling!), serve a fruit dessert of your choice.
- Any left-over cheese fondue can be chilled and used in soups, as a filling for potatoes baked in their skins or in tomato-based sauces.
- Remember all fondues are very hot, so take care not to burn the mouth.

MEAT, FISH & SEAFOOD FONDUES

- Fondues such as Mongolian Chicken Hot Pot that are cooked in simmering stock require pots that transmit heat quickly and keep the cooking liquid at its highest temperature. The pots should be filled to just over half full. Take care not to overfill.
- When using oil, the temperature should be around 180 to 190°C (350 to 375°F). If no thermometer is available, drop a small cube of bread into the oil. The bread will turn golden in about 30 seconds if the oil is at the correct temperature.
- Unless otherwise specified, use a vegetable oil of your choice.
- If liked, a little flavoured oil can be added to the basic cooking oil.
- For meat or fish, choose good-quality meat that cooks quickly and firm fish that will not disintegrate during cooking. These fondues are much enhanced when served with dips and sauces in which the cooked food can be rolled before eating.
- To prevent the food spitting, meat and fish should be dried before cooking in the hot oil. If too much food is put into the hot oil at any one time, it will lower the temperature and you may find the oil will need reheating on the stove.

DESSERT FONDUES

- If you do not have a specific chocolate fondue pot (these have a maximum chocolate fill level and are a slightly different shape from usual pots), then any fondue pot will work well for desserts.
- As a general rule, do not boil dessert fondues as this will impair the flavour; they are designed to be eaten warm, not hot. Remember chocolate burns very easily.
- If you chill fresh fruit dippers before serving, you will find the chocolate will coat the fruit more easily.

Eating fondue should be fun—so browse through the recipes in this book and pick out a few tempting ideas to try, invite some friends over and enjoy a great, fun-packed, delicious informal party.

FISH & SEAFOOD

THAI JUMBO PRAWN FONDUE

THIS IS A FONDUE WITH A DIFFERENCE—HERE THE PRAWNS ARE COOKED IN A STOCK, THEN BEAN SPROUTS AND NOODLES ARE ADDED AT THE END OF COOKING.

Devein the prawns, rinse lightly and pat dry with kitchen paper. Place in small bowls, garnish with lime wedges and sprigs of fresh coriander, cover and leave in the fridge.

Place the ginger, lemon grass, chillies, garlic, lime zest and stock in a Mongolian hot pot and bring to the boil. Simmer for 15 minutes then stir in the chopped coriander. Place over the lit spirit stove.

Combine all the ingredients for the dipping sauce and set aside.

Cook the noodles in boiling water for 3 minutes or until cooked, drain and set aside.

Spear the prawns on to the forks and cook for 1 to 2 minutes in the hot stock then dip into the dipping sauce before eating.

When all the prawns have been cooked, add the noodles and bean sprouts to the pot, heat for 1 to 2 minutes, then ladle into soup bowls and serve as soup.

Serves **6**
Preparation time **5 minutes**
Cooking time **20 to 22 minutes**

900 g/2 lb raw king-size prawns, peeled
1 Tbsp grated fresh root ginger
2 stalks lemon grass
1 to 3 chillies, deseeded and chopped
2 to 3 garlic cloves, peeled
Grated zest of $\frac{1}{2}$ lime
750 ml/1¼ pt fish stock or water
3 Tbsp chopped fresh coriander
75 g/3 oz dried thread egg noodles
50 g/2 oz bean sprouts

DIPPING SAUCE
1 Tbsp soy sauce
2 tsp fish sauce or $\frac{1}{2}$ tsp salt
2 tsp clear honey, warmed
1 Thai chilli, deseeded and chopped

TO GARNISH
Lime wedges and fresh coriander sprigs

CRISPY SCAMPI FONDUE

SCAMPI CAN BE QUITE DIFFICULT TO SKEWER ON TO THE FONDUE FORK: TRY SKEWERING THREE TO FOUR AT A TIME BEFORE COOKING.

Devein the scampi, rinse lightly, dry thoroughly on kitchen paper and set aside. Mix together the lemon zest, chillies, flour and seasoning. Roll the scampi in the flour mixture and leave for at least 30 minutes.

Place the beaten egg and the breadcrumbs in two separate shallow dishes. Dip the scampi in the beaten egg, allowing any excess egg to drip back into the bowl, then coat in the breadcrumbs. Place in a serving bowl and garnish with parsley sprigs.

Heat the oil in the fondue pot then transfer the pot to the lighted spirit stove in order to keep it hot.

Each guest can now spear the scampi with their forks and cook them in the hot oil for 1 to 2 minutes or until golden and crisp. Serve with the Tartare Sauce, lemon wedges and pitta bread filled with lettuce, cucumber and cherry tomatoes.

Serves **4 as a main course or 8 as a starter**
Preparation time **10 minutes plus 30 minutes marinating time**
Cooking time **2 to 3 minutes per piece**

450 g/1 lb raw king-size prawns, peeled
2 Tbsp lemon zest
1½ tsp dried crushed chillies
2 Tbsp plain white flour
Salt and freshly ground black pepper
2 medium eggs, beaten
50 g/2 oz dried breadcrumbs
600 ml/1 pt oil, for frying

TO GARNISH
Parsley sprigs

TO SERVE
Tartare sauce *(see page 100)*, **lemon wedges, warm pitta bread filled with shredded lettuce, cucumber strips and quartered cherry tomatoes**

DRUNKEN HADDOCK FONDUE

LOOK FOR THICK FILLETS OF FISH FOR THIS FONDUE AND CUT INTO THICK CUBES.

Serves **4 to 6**
Preparation time **35 minutes**
Cooking time **2 to 3 minutes** **per piece**

675 g/1½ lb smoked haddock fillets, skinned and bones discarded (reserve the trimmings)
1 large carrot
1 medium onion
1 small bunch fresh herbs
A few black peppercorns
250 ml/8 fl oz dry white wine
475 ml/16 fl oz water

TO GARNISH
Lemon wedges and fresh chervil sprigs

TO SERVE
Creamy Herb Mayonnaise (see page 104), warm crusty bread and assorted salads

Rinse the fish and pat dry. Cut into large cubes or strips. Place the fish in small bowls, garnish with lemon wedges and chervil, cover and chill until required.

Peel and slice the carrot and onion, and place in a large pan with the fish trimmings, herbs, peppercorns, wine and water. Bring to the boil and simmer for at least 30 minutes. Strain into the fondue pot and place on the lighted spirit stove.

Spear the fish on to the fondue forks and cook in the hot stock for 2 to 3 minutes. Serve with the mayonnaise, bread and salads.

ASIAN FISH HOT POT FONDUE

USE AN ASSORTMENT OF FISH THAT PROVIDE A GOOD VARIETY OF COLOURS AND TEXTURES.

Serves **6**
Preparation time **15 minutes**
Cooking time **22 to 23 minutes**

900 g/2 lb assorted fish fillet such as cod, salmon, monkfish and scallops
1 large carrot, peeled and sliced
1 large onion, peeled and sliced
2 bird's-eye chillies, deseeded and sliced
A few fresh parsley sprigs
4 star anise
1 tsp whole peppercorns
1 Tbsp grated fresh root ginger
750 ml/1¼ pt water
4 Tbsp dry sherry
1 Tbsp soy sauce

TO GARNISH
Fresh coriander sprigs and lime wedges

TO SERVE
Glutinous (short grain) rice and Mixed Chinese Green Salad (see page 108)

Skin the fish, reserving the trimmings, and discard any bones. Clean scallops if using. Cut the fish into cubes, place in small bowls and garnish with coriander sprigs and lime wedges. Cover and chill until required.

Place the carrot, onion and chillies in the Mongolian hot pot with the fish trimmings, the parsley, remaining spices and the water. Bring to the boil, then simmer for 20 minutes or until the stock has reduced by about one-third. Strain and return to the pot, then stir in the sherry and soy sauce.

Heat the stock, then place over the lighted spirit stove, and gently simmer.

Spear the fish on to the fondue forks, cook in the stocks for 2 to 3 minutes. Serve with the rice and salad.

SALMON LAKSA FONDUE

THIS FONDUE PROVIDES AN INTERESTING AND FUN MEAL THAT BOTH FRIENDS AND FAMILY WILL LOVE. THE AROMATIC FLAVOURS OF THE ASIAN SPICES GENTLY PERFUME THE SALMON AS IT COOKS IN THE COCONUT MILK.

Place the coconut milk with the chillies, fresh root ginger, lemon grass, star anise, shallots and carrot in a pan and simmer gently for 15 minutes. Remove from the heat and allow to infuse for 15 minutes, then strain into the fondue pot.

Place the fondue pot over the lighted spirit stove and allow to heat through. Discard any bones from the salmon, rinse lightly and pat dry on kitchen paper. Cut into cubes.

Mix the coriander and cornflour together then use to coat the salmon. Leave to marinate for 45 minutes.

Spear the salmon on to fondue forks or wooden skewers and cook in the flavoured coconut mix for 2 to 3 minutes. Serve with the Mixed Chinese Green Salad.

Serves **4 to 6**
Preparation time **6 to 8 minutes plus 15 minutes infusing time and 45 minutes marinating time**
Cooking time **2 to 3 minutes per piece**

600 ml/1 pt unsweetened coconut milk
2 bird's-eye chillies, deseeded and chopped
1 Tbsp grated fresh root ginger
2 stalks lemon grass, chopped
3 to 4 star anise
3 to 4 shallots, peeled and chopped
1 large carrot, grated
550 g/1 lb 4 oz fresh salmon fillet, skinned
2 Tbsp chopped fresh coriander
2 Tbsp cornflour

TO SERVE
Mixed Chinese Green Salad *(see page 108)*

BOSTON CHOWDER FONDUE

AN IDEAL SUPPER TO SERVE WHEN YOU WISH TO HAVE AN INFORMAL GATHERING—FRESH OR CANNED CLAMS WORK WELL IN THIS FONDUE. IF USING FRESH CLAMS, PREPARE AND COOK THEM BEFORE USE.

Serves **6**
Preparation time **5 minutes**
Cooking time **8 to 10 minutes**

50 g/2 oz butter
8 spring onions, trimmed and chopped
6 Tbsp plain white flour
350 ml/12 fl oz milk
550 g/1¼ lb tinned or live clams,
 freshly cooked
125 ml/4 fl oz clam juice (if using tinned clams)
3 Tbsp lemon juice
100 g/4 oz sweetcorn
2 Tbsp chopped fresh parsley
A few drops of Tabasco Sauce
Salt and freshly ground black pepper

TO SERVE
Cooked baby new potatoes, strips of red and
 green pepper and celery stalks for dipping

Place the butter in the fondue pot over a gentle heat and cook, stirring until melted. Add the spring onions and cook for 2 minutes. Stir in the flour and cook for 2 minutes.

Gradually stir in the milk, bring to the boil and simmer for 2 minutes. Drain the clams if using canned, reserving the liquor, then stir the liquor into the pot with the lemon juice, sweetcorn, parsley, Tabasco Sauce and seasoning. Cook for 2 to 3 minutes or until the sweetcorn is cooked.

Stir in the clams, place the pot over the lighted spirit stove and cook for a few minutes to heat through. Serve with potatoes, pepper strips and celery stalks.

SOLE & ORANGE FONDUE

SOLE IS A DELICATE FISH AND REQUIRES ONLY THE MINIMUM OF COOKING. LEAVE THE SKIN ON THE FISH AND CUT INTO STRIPS SO IT CAN BE THREADED ON TO THE FONDUE FORKS AND WILL NOT FALL OFF INTO THE POT DURING COOKING.

Serves **4**
Preparation time **8 to 10 minutes plus**
 30 minutes marinating time
Cooking time **1 to 2 minutes per piece**

675 g/1½ lb sole fillets
Grated zest of 1 large orange
4 Tbsp orange juice
1 Tbsp liquid orange
 blossom honey, warmed
2 tsp cornflour
Salt and freshly ground black pepper
600 ml/1 pt sunflower oil, for frying

TO GARNISH
Orange wedges and tarragon sprigs

TO SERVE
Freshly cooked baby new potatoes,
 Green Mayonnaise *(see page 96)*
 and Avocado & Mango Salad
 (see page 106)

Rinse the fish lightly and pat dry on kitchen paper. Cut into strips and place aside.

Mix the orange zest, juice, honey, cornflour and seasoning together and pour over the sole strips. Leave to marinate for 30 minutes. Place in small bowls and garnish with orange wedges and tarragon sprigs.

Heat the oil in the fondue pot, then transfer to the lighted spirit stove.

Thread the sole strips on to the fondue forks and cook in the hot oil for 1 to 2 minutes, or until crisp. Serve with the potatoes, salad and mayonnaise.

CRISPY SMOKED FISH FONDUE

THIS IS AN IDEAL FONDUE TO PREPARE AHEAD, LEAVING YOU PLENTY OF TIME TO ENJOY ENTERTAINING YOUR GUESTS.

Discard the skin from the fish and flake into small pieces. Set aside.

Melt the butter in a small pan, then stir in the flour and cook for 2 minutes. Take off the heat and gradually stir in the milk, then return to the heat and cook, stirring until thick and glossy.

Remove from the heat and stir in the reserved fish, the lemon zest, anchovy essence, spring onions and parsley. Mix lightly, then turn into a bowl, cover lightly and chill for at least 30 minutes, longer if time permits.

Place the egg and breadcrumbs in two separate shallow bowls. Form the chilled fish mixture into small balls, then dip into the beaten egg, allowing any excess to drip back into the bowl and then coat in the breadcrumbs. Chill until required.

Heat the oil in the fondue pot, then place over the lighted spirit stove. Spear the fish balls on to skewers and cook in the hot oil for 2 to 3 minutes or until crisp. Garnish with the lemon wedges and serve with the Tartare Sauce, coleslaw and chips.

Serves **4 to 6**
Preparation time **15 minutes plus**
 30 minutes marinating time
Cooking time **2 to 3 minutes per piece**
 plus 5 minutes for sauce

350 g/12 oz smoked mackerel fillet
50 g/2 oz butter
50 g/2 oz plain white flour
250 ml/8 fl oz milk
Grated zest of 1 lemon
1 tsp anchovy essence
6 spring onions, finely chopped
1 Tbsp chopped fresh parsley
2 medium eggs, beaten
100 g/4 oz dried natural white
 breadcrumbs
600 ml/1 pt oil, for frying

TO GARNISH
Lemon wedges

TO SERVE
Tartare Sauce *(see page 100)*, **Zesty Orange Coleslaw** *(see page 114)* **and chips**

MIXED FISH FONDUE

COATING THE FISH IN CORNFLOUR HELPS KEEP THE
FLESH TOGETHER WHILST COOKING.

Serves **6 to 8**
Preparation time **15 minutes**
   plus 15 minutes marinating time
Cooking time **2 to 4 minutes per piece**

900 g/2 lb assorted fish such as
   monkfish, salmon, cod, jumbo
   prawns and scallops
2 large egg whites
2 to 3 tsp Tabasco Sauce, or to taste
2 to 3 Tbsp chopped fresh coriander
3 Tbsp cornflour
600 ml/1 pt oil, for frying

TO GARNISH
Parsley sprigs and lemon
   wedges

TO SERVE
Soured Cream Sauce *(see*
   page 103), **Artichoke & Bean**
   Salad with Vinaigrette
   (see page 110) **and freshly**
   cooked rice

Trim the fish, discarding any bones. Peel and devein the prawns if
using. Rinse lightly and dry on kitchen paper. Cut into cubes and
place in a shallow dish.

Beat the egg whites, then stir in the Tabasco Sauce and coriander.
Place the cornflour into a bowl, then beat in the egg white mixture.

Pour the egg white mixture over the fish and stir lightly until coated.
Cover and chill for 15 minutes. Place on a serving platter and
garnish with parsley and lemon wedges.

Heat the oil, then pour into the fondue pot. Place over the lighted
spirit stove. Spear the fish on to the fondue forks and cook for 2 to 3
minutes, then serve with the Soured Cream Sauce, Artichoke & Bean
Salad with Vinaigrette and rice.

TUNA & TOMATO FONDUE

THIS FONDUE MAKES A SUBSTANTIAL MEAL WHEN SERVED WITH WARM BREAD OR JACKET POTATOES AND A TOSSED GREEN SALAD.

Serves **4**
Preparation time **10 minutes**
Cooking time **22 to 25 minutes,**
    plus 2 minutes for each piece of tuna

450 g/1 lb fresh tuna steak
Fresh basil sprigs
1 Tbsp olive oil
1 small onion, chopped
2 to 3 garlic cloves, peeled and crushed
450 g/1 lb ripe tomatoes, skinned
1 Tbsp tomato paste
2 Tbsp water
120 ml/4 fl oz white wine

120 ml/4 fl oz water
Basil sprigs
Salt and freshly ground black pepper
1 red and 1 yellow pepper, deseeded
    and cubed
1 large courgette, cubed

TO GARNISH
Basil sprigs

TO SERVE
Warm crusty bread or potatoes baked in
    their skins, Green Tomatillo Sauce *(see page 100)*
    and Tossed Green Salad *(see page 114)*

Cut the tuna into cubes, place in small bowls with a few basil sprigs, cover and chill.

Heat the oil in a pan and sauté the onion and garlic for 5 minutes or until softened.

Chop the tomatoes and add to the pan with the tomato paste, blended with 2 tablespoons of water. Cook for 5 minutes then add the wine, water, 2 to 3 sprigs of basil, and seasoning to taste. Bring to the boil, then simmer for 10 to 15 minutes or until a thick sauce is formed.

Purée in a food processor, adjust seasoning, then pour into the fondue pot and place over the lighted spirit stove. Heat through. Dip the peppers and courgettes in boiling water, then drain. Arrange in small bowls and garnish with a few basil sprigs.

Spear the tuna and vegetable cubes on to the fondue forks and cook in the tomato sauce. Serve with bread or potatoes, Green Tomatillo Sauce and the salad.

SEAFOOD & CHEESE FONDUE

USE WHICHEVER SEAFOOD YOU PREFER FOR THIS DELICIOUS CREAMY FONDUE—SHELLFISH GO REALLY
WELL WITH THE CHEESE AND A CRISP, CHILLED CHARDONNAY IS AN EXCELLENT ACCOMPANIMENT.

Place the garlic, chilli and white wine in a pan, bring to the boil and simmer for 3 minutes. Discard the garlic and chilli, pour the wine into the fondue pan and add the sherry and lime juice. Place over the lighted spirit stove.

Mix the cheese and cornflour together, then gradually add to the fondue pot, stirring continuously until the cheese has melted.

Stir in the chopped spring onions and parsley, and heat gently. Spear the fish on to the fondue forks and dip into the fondue until well coated in the cheese and heated through. Garnish with the lemon wedges and serve with the rye bread, dipping sauces and salads.

Serves **3 to 4**
Preparation time **12 to 15 minutes**
Cooking time **5 to 7 minutes**

1 garlic clove, peeled
1 serrano chilli, deseeded and chopped
250 ml/8 fl oz dry white wine
2 Tbsp dry sherry
1 Tbsp lime juice
175 g/6 oz Emmental cheese, grated
1 Tbsp cornflour
4 spring onions, trimmed and chopped
1 Tbsp chopped fresh parsley
450 g/1 lb assorted seafish such as cubes of cooked lobster meat, cooked peeled king-size prawns, cooked green-lipped mussels and pieces of smoked mackerel

TO GARNISH
Lemon wedges

TO SERVE
Rye bread for dipping, Green Tomatillo Sauce *(see page 100)*, Creamy Herb Mayonnaise *(see page 104)*, Chilled Ratatouille *(see page 109)* and Tossed Green Salad *(see page 114)*

PRAWN SATAY FONDUE

THIS RECIPE WOULD ALSO WORK REALLY WELL WITH CUBES OF CHICKEN OR TURKEY, OR A MIXTURE OF ALL THREE—PRAWNS, CHICKEN AND TURKEY. BE SURE TO SERVE PLENTY OF SATAY SAUCE AS IT IS AN ALL-TIME FAVOURITE.

Devein the prawns, then split along the inner side and flatten to form a butterfly shape. Set aside.

Warm the peanut butter, then gradually stir in the coconut milk to form a creamy sauce. Stir in the garlic, lime and chillies, and mix lightly. Pour over the prawn, cover and leave in the fridge for at least 30 minutes. Stir occasionally during marinating.

Heat the oil in the fondue pot, then place on the lighted spirit stove.

Drain the prawns and spear on to fondue forks, then cook in the hot oil for 2 to 3 minutes or until cooked. Serve with the Satay Sauce and salads.

Serves **4**
Preparation time **10 minutes plus
   30 minutes marinating time**
Cooking time **2 to 3 minutes per piece**

450 g/1 lb raw king-size prawns
3 Tbsp smooth or crunchy peanut butter
120 ml/4 fl oz coconut milk
2 to 3 garlic cloves, crushed
Grated zest of 1 lime
**2 bird's-eye chillies, deseeded and
   chopped**
600 ml/1 pt peanut oil, for frying

TO SERVE

Satay Sauce *(see page 99)*, **Mixed Chinese
   Green Salad** *(see page 108)* **and Spiced
   Rice Salad** *(see page 109)*

MEAT

CAJUN BEEF FONDUE

DRY SPICE RUBS ARE USED BOTH IN CAJUN AND CARIBBEAN COOKING. YOU CAN INCREASE OR DECREASE THE AMOUNT OF SPICES USED, ACCORDING TO PERSONAL PREFERENCE.

Trim the steak and set aside. Mix together the dry marinade ingredients and rub over the steak. Place on a plate, cover lightly, and leave in the fridge for at least 30 minutes.

Heat the oil in the fondue pot to 190°C/375°F, then place on the lighted spirit stove.

Cut the steak into strips, then thread on to the skewers or fondue forks. Cook in the hot oil for 2 to 5 minutes or until cooked to personal preference.

Garnish with the thyme sprigs, and serve with the Soured Cream Sauce, salad, sweet potatoes and braised okra.

Serves **4 to 6**

Preparation time **5 minutes plus 30 minutes marinating time**

Cooking time **2 to 5 minutes per strip**

550 g/1¼ lb sirloin steak
¼ tsp dried red pepper flakes
¼ to ½ tsp cayenne pepper
½ tsp sugar
¼ to ½ tsp salt
¼ tsp freshly ground black pepper
2 Tbsp chopped fresh thyme
2 to 3 garlic cloves, peeled and crushed
600 ml/1 pt oil, for frying

TO GARNISH
Fresh thyme sprigs

TO SERVE
Soured Cream Sauce *(see page 103)*, **Tossed Green Salad** *(see page 114)*, **caramelized sweet potatoes and braised okra**

FONDUE BOURGUIGNONNE

PERHAPS THE MOST WELL KNOWN OF ALL FONDUES, ORIGINATING IN FRANCE, BUT NOW ENJOYED IN MANY DIFFERENT COUNTRIES.

Cut the steak into cubes, place in individual dishes and garnish with the parsley sprigs and tomato wedges.

Deseed and chop the tomatoes into small dice, then place in a small bowl. Place the shallots and parsley in small dishes. Add the garlic clove and bay leaf into the oil, heat in the fondue pot to 190°C/375°F, then carefully transfer to the lighted spirit stove.

Spear the meat on to the fondue forks and cook in the oil for 1 to 4 minutes, until cooked to personal preference. Once cooked, roll in any or all of the tomatoes, shallots and parsley. Serve with the creamed horseradish, olives, chutney, dipping sauce and bread.

Serves **6 to 8**
Preparation time **10 minutes**
Cooking time **1 to 4 minutes per cube**

900 g/2 lb fillet or sirloin steak
4 tomatoes
4 shallots, peeled and chopped
3 Tbsp chopped fresh parsley
600 ml/1 pt oil, for frying
1 garlic clove, peeled
1 fresh bay leaf

TO GARNISH
Fresh parsley sprigs and tomato wedges

TO SERVE
Creamed horseradish, olives, fruit
  chutney, Green Tomatillo Sauce
  (see page 100) **and crusty bread**

TURKISH KEBABS FONDUE

SPICES BECOME STALE QUITE QUICKLY SO ALWAYS STORE THEM IN A COOL DARK PLACE. FOR BEST RESULTS, USE THE FRESHEST SPICES AVAILABLE AND GRIND THEM WITH A PESTLE AND MORTAR JUST BEFORE YOU NEED THEM.

Mix together the minced beef, spices, onion, garlic, lemon zest, coriander and seasoning to taste. Form into small balls about the size of a cherry tomato. Place on a serving plate, garnish with the coriander sprigs, and sprinkle with the spring onions.

Heat the oil in the fondue pot to 190°C/375°F and place carefully on the lighted spirit stove.

Spear the meatballs on to fondue forks or skewers, fry in the oil and serve with the Indian-style Raita and salads.

Serves **4 to 6**
Preparation time **10 minutes**
Cooking time **2 to 5 minutes**
  per meatball

450 g/1 lb minced beef
1½ tsp ground coriander
1½ tsp ground cumin
1 small onion, peeled and chopped
3 to 4 garlic cloves, peeled and crushed
1 Tbsp grated lemon zest
2 Tbsp chopped fresh coriander
Salt and freshly ground black pepper
600 ml/1 pt oil, for frying

TO GARNISH
Coriander sprigs and chopped spring onions

TO SERVE
Indian-style Raita *(see page 104)*, **Tossed Green Salad** *(see page 114)* **and Mint and Lemon Tabbouleh** *(see page 118)*

SWEET & SOUR BEEF FONDUE

ONE OF THE JOYS IN HOSTING A FONDUE PARTY IS THAT IT CAN BE AS EASY OR AS COMPLICATED AS YOU WISH. MOST OF THIS FONDUE CAN BE PREPARED WELL AHEAD OF TIME: MARINATING THE MEAT OVERNIGHT WILL ENSURE THAT IT WILL SIMPLY MELT IN THE MOUTH. THE BATTER, DIPPING SAUCE AND SALAD CAN QUICKLY BE MADE JUST BEFORE THEY ARE REQUIRED—THEN ALL YOU HAVE TO DO IS RELAX AND ENJOY THE OCCASION WITH YOUR FRIENDS.

Cut the steak into cubes and place in a shallow dish. Mix together the garlic, sugar, soy sauce, vinegar and wine, and pour over the meat. Stir and cover. Leave to marinate in the fridge for at least 30 minutes, stirring occasionally during marinating to ensure the meat is fully coated.

Mix the eggs and water together until light and frothy, then sift in the flour and cornflour (do not worry if there are a few lumps). Place in small bowls.

Drain the meat and place in small bowls. Garnish with coriander sprigs.

Heat the oil to 190°C/375°F in the fondue pot, then carefully place on the lighted spirit stove. Spear a piece of meat on to a fondue fork, dip the meat in the batter then fry it in the oil until the batter is crisp and golden. Serve with the dipping sauce, salad, rice and mango chutney.

Serves **6**
Preparation time **10 minutes plus 30 minutes marinating time**
Cooking time **2 to 4 minutes per piece**

675 g/1½ lb fillet or sirloin steak
3 to 4 garlic cloves, peeled and crushed
1 Tbsp granulated brown sugar
2 Tbsp soy sauce
2 Tbsp red wine vinegar
250 ml/8 fl oz red wine

FOR THE BATTER
2 medium eggs, beaten
250 ml/8 fl oz ice-cold water
100 g/4 oz plain white flour
50 g/2 oz cornflour
600 ml/1 pt oil, for frying

TO GARNISH
Chopped fresh coriander

TO SERVE
Sweet & Sour Sauce *(see page 97)*, Mint & Lemon Tabbouleh *(see page 118)*, fresh cooked rice and mango chutney

BEEF IN RED WINE FONDUE

WHEN COOKING WITH WINE, ALWAYS USE THE BEST YOU CAN
AFFORD—YOU WILL CERTAINLY NOT REGRET IT.

Serves **6**
Preparation time **8 to 10 minutes**
  plus 30 minutes marinating time
Cooking time **1 to 2 minutes per piece**

900 g/2 lb rump or sirloin steak,
  trimmed and cubed
3 to 5 garlic cloves, peeled and
  finely sliced
4 to 5 shallots, peeled and chopped
1 Tbsp granulated brown sugar
2 Tbsp chopped fresh parsley
350 ml/12 fl oz red wine, such as
  Bordeaux
600 ml/1 pt oil, for frying

TO GARNISH
Fresh parsley sprigs

TO SERVE
Avocado & Mango Salad *(see page 106)*,
  Artichoke Heart Salad *(see page 115)*
  and crusty bread

Place the steak in a shallow dish. Scatter over the garlic, shallots, sugar
and parsley, then pour over the red wine. Cover and leave in the fridge for
at least 30 minutes. Spoon the marinade over the steak occasionally.

When ready to cook, drain the steak, reserving the marinade, and arrange
the steak in small dishes. Garnish with parsley sprigs.

Strain, then boil the marinade vigorously for about 10 minutes or until it is
reduced by half and has become syrupy. Pour into small dishes and use as
a dipping sauce.

Heat the oil to 190°C/375°F in the fondue pot then place over the lighted
spirit stove. Spear the meat on to the fondue forks and cook according to
taste. Serve with the salads and bread.

CHILLI MEATBALL FONDUE

CHILLIES CAN VARY TREMENDOUSLY IN BOTH FLAVOUR AND HEAT INTENSITY. I HAVE SUGGESTED RED SERRANO CHILLIES, AS THEY ARE A PARTICULAR FAVOURITE OF MINE. HOWEVER, YOU MAY PREFER TO SUBSTITUTE ANOTHER VARIETY.

Serves **4**
Preparation time **10 minutes**
Cooking time **3 to 5 minutes**
  per meatball

450 g/1 lb minced beef
1 small onion, grated
2 to 3 garlic cloves, peeled and crushed
1 to 2 red serrano chillies, deseeded and
  finely chopped
1 Tbsp tomato purée
Salt and freshly ground black pepper
1 Tbsp chopped fresh oregano
600 ml/1 pt oil, for frying

TO GARNISH
**Pickled chillies and fresh oregano
sprigs**

TO SERVE
**Warm pitta breads, shredded lettuce
and Green Tomatillo Sauce** *(see
page 100)*

Mix together the minced beef, onion, garlic, chillies, tomato purée, seasoning and chopped oregano. With dampened hands, form into small meatballs the size of a large cherry. Place on a serving plate and garnish with pickled chillies and fresh oregano sprigs.

Heat the oil to 190°C/375°F in the fondue pot and place over the lighted spirit stove. Spear the meatballs on to fondue forks or skewers and cook in the hot oil for 3 to 5 minutes or until cooked.

Split the pitta bread and fill with some shredded lettuce, place the cooked meatballs in the pitta and drizzle with some Green Tomatillo Sauce to serve.

APRICOT & MINT LAMB FONDUE

THIS IS ALSO GOOD SERVED WITH WARM, CRISP TACO SHELLS. SIMPLY FILL THE SHELLS WITH SHREDDED LETTUCE AND TOP WITH THE MEATBALLS AND CUCUMBER.

Serves **4 to 6**
Preparation time **10 minutes**
Cooking time **3 to 5 minutes per meatball**

450 g/1 lb minced lamb

75 g/3 oz ready-to-eat dried apricots, finely chopped

2 to 3 garlic cloves, peeled and crushed

1 small red onion, finely chopped

2 Tbsp chopped fresh mint

Salt and freshly ground pepper

600 ml/1 pt oil, for frying

TO GARNISH

Mint sprigs and fresh apricot slices

TO SERVE

**Warm split pitta breads, shredded lettuce, grated
  cucumber and Green Mayonnaise** *(see page 96)*

Place the minced lamb with the apricots, garlic,
onion, mint and seasoning in a bowl and mix well.
Form into small balls about the size of a small
cherry tomato. Place on a plate and garnish with
mint sprigs and apricot slices.

Heat the oil in the fondue pot and place over
the lighted spirit stove. Spear on to the fondue
forks or skewers and cook in the hot oil for 3 to
5 minutes or until cooked.

Split the pitta breads, fill with lettuce, cucumber
and meatballs, and serve with the mayonnaise.

BEEF & HORSERADISH FONDUE

IF YOU CAN FIND FRESH HORSERADISH, USE IT IN THIS
RECIPE AS THE FLAVOUR IS SUPERB. IF NOT, USE GRATED
OR CREAMED HORSERADISH.

Serves **4**
Preparation time **5 to 7 minutes**
  plus 30 minutes marinating time
Cooking time **2 to 4 minutes per strip**

550 g/1¼ lb sirloin or rump steak

1 to 2 Tbsp grated or creamed horseradish

4 Tbsp olive oil

2 Tbsp red wine vinegar

Salt and freshly ground black pepper

600 ml/1 pt oil, for frying

TO GARNISH

Flat-leaf parsley

TO SERVE

**Creamed horseradish sauce,
  Sauerkraut** *(see page 107)*,
  **Creamy Potato and Apple
  Salad** *(see page 117)* **and
  crusty bread**

Trim and cut the steak into strips, and place in a shallow dish.
Mix together the horseradish, oil, vinegar and seasoning, then pour over
the beef. Stir, cover lightly and leave to marinate in the fridge for at
least 30 minutes. Stir occasionally during this time.

Heat the oil in the fondue pot to 190°C/375°F, then carefully place over
the lighted spirit stove. Drain the beef and spear on to the fondue forks.
Cook in the hot oil for 2 to 4 minutes or according to personal taste.
Garnish with the flat-leaf parsley, and serve with the sauce, salads
and bread.

SICILIAN LAMB FONDUE

WHEN MARINATING FOODS, THE LONGER THE MARINATING TIME, THE BETTER THE FLAVOUR. WITH MEAT, LEAVING IT FOR LONGER NOT ONLY IMPROVES THE TASTE, BUT ALSO HELPS TO MAKE THE MEAT MORE SUCCULENT.

Cut the lamb into strips and place in a shallow dish. Scatter over the garlic, onion, thyme, spices and sugar.

Blend the tomato purée, Marsala wine and lemon juice together and pour over the lamb. Stir, cover and leave to marinate in the fridge for at least 30 minutes, or longer if time permits.

Drain the lamb, reserving the marinade. Arrange the lamb in small dishes, and garnish with the thyme sprigs.

Boil the marinade rapidly until it is reduced by half and has become syrupy, then pour into small dishes and use as a dipping sauce.

Heat the oil in the fondue pot, then place over the lighted spirit stove. Thread the lamb on to the fondue forks and cook in the hot oil for 2 to 3 minutes or until cooked to personal preference. Roll in the toasted chopped almonds and serve with the Green Mayonnaise, salads and bread.

Serves **4 to 6**
Preparation time **8 to 10 minutes** plus 30 minutes marinating time
Cooking time **2 to 3 minutes** per piece

675 g/1½ lb lean lamb fillet
2 to 3 garlic cloves, crushed
1 large onion, chopped
2 Tbsp chopped fresh thyme
1 tsp cumin seeds, toasted
1 tsp ground cardamom
2 Tbsp dark brown sugar
1 Tbsp tomato purée
250 ml/8 fl oz Marsala wine
3 Tbsp lemon juice
600 ml/1 pt oil, for frying

TO GARNISH
Fresh thyme sprigs

TO SERVE
Toasted chopped flaked almonds, Green Mayonnaise *(see page 96)*, **Chilled Ratatouille** *(see page 109)*, **Spicy Pepper & Mushroom Salad** *(see page 116)* **and warm Italian-style bread such as focaccia**

ROSEMARY-SCENTED LAMB FONDUE

LAMB, ROSEMARY AND GARLIC ARE A WINNING COMBINATION, AND THE ADDITION OF THE APPLE JUICE ADDS A DELICIOUS TANG.

Serves **6**
Preparation time **10 minutes plus 30 minutes marinating time**
Cooking time **2 to 3 minutes per piece**

675 g/1½ lb lean lamb, cut into thin strips
3 to 4 garlic cloves, peeled and crushed
8 spring onions, trimmed and chopped
2 Tbsp chopped fresh rosemary
2 Tbsp light soy sauce
250 ml/8 fl oz apple juice
600 ml/1 pt oil, for frying

TO GARNISH
Rosemary sprigs and wedges of
    dessert apples

TO SERVE
Soured Cream Sauce *(see page 103)*,
    Spiced Rice Salad *(see page 109)*,
    Tossed Green Salad *(see page 114)*
    and crusty bread

Place the strips of lamb in a shallow dish, then scatter over the garlic, spring onions and rosemary.

Blend the soy sauce with the apple juice, then pour the liquid over the lamb and stir lightly. Cover and leave to marinate in the fridge for at least 30 minutes. Stir occasionally.

Heat the oil in the fondue pot and carefully place on the lighted spirit stove.

Drain the lamb and boil the marinade vigorously until reduced by half. Serve in small bowls as a dipping sauce.

Thread the lamb on to the fondue forks and cook in the hot oil for 2 to 3 minutes. Garnish with the rosemary and apple wedges, and serve with the Soured Cream Sauce, salads and crusty bread.

Marinated Pork & Orange Fondue

MARINATED PORK & ORANGE FONDUE

MARRYING SAVOURY DISHES WITH FRUIT IS A PARTICULAR FAVOURITE OF MINE—AS IN THIS DELICIOUS COMBINATION.

Serves **4**
Preparation time **10 minutes plus**
30 minutes marinating time
Cooking time **3 to 4 minutes per piece**

450 g/1 lb pork fillet, cubed
1 medium onion, chopped
1 to 2 garlic cloves, peeled and crushed
2 Tbsp grated orange zest
120 ml/4 fl oz orange juice
2 tsp granulated brown sugar
1 Tbsp light soy sauce
3 Tbsp walnut oil
2 Tbsp chopped fresh sage
600 ml/1 pt groundnut oil, for frying

TO GARNISH
Fresh sage leaves, orange wedges

TO SERVE
Cooked new potatoes, Orange Cumberland Dipping Sauce (see page 102) and Zesty Orange Coleslaw (see page 114)

Place the pork in a shallow dish, then scatter with onion and garlic.

Mix together the orange zest, juice, sugar, soy sauce, walnut oil and sage, then pour over the pork. Cover and leave to marinate in the fridge for at least 30 minutes.

Drain the pork, reserving the marinade, and place the pork in individual dishes garnished with the sage leaves and orange wedges.

Boil the marinade rapidly until reduced by half, pour into small bowls and serve as a dipping sauce. Heat the oil in the fondue pot, then carefully place over the lighted spirit stove. Spear the pork on to fondue forks and cook in the hot oil. Serve with the potatoes, Orange Cumberland Dipping Sauce and coleslaw.

ASIAN FRUITY PORK FONDUE

YOU CAN BUY DIFFERENT TYPES OF MANGO CHUTNEY—SOME ARE MILD WHILE OTHERS HAVE QUITE A BITE TO THEM. CHOOSE WHICHEVER YOU PREFER, BUT CHOP THE LARGER PIECES OF CHUTNEY BEFORE USING.

Place the minced pork in a bowl and add the mango chutney, chillies, garlic, shallots and coriander. Mix together then form into small balls about the size of a large cherry. Place on a serving plate and garnish with the fruit and chopped coriander.

Heat the oil in the fondue pot, then carefully transfer to the lighted spirit stove. Spear the meatballs on to skewers or fondue forks and cook in the heated oil for 3 to 5 minutes or until cooked.

Serve with the glutinous (short-grain) rice, Sweet & Sour Sauce, pineapple, peppers and mango chutney.

Serves **6**
Preparation time **10 minutes**
Cooking time **3 to 5 minutes**
   per meatball

675g/1½ lb minced pork
3 Tbsp mango chutney
2 jalapeño chillies, peeled and finely
   chopped
2 to 3 garlic cloves, peeled and crushed
4 shallots, peeled and chopped
2 Tbsp chopped fresh coriander
600 ml/1 pt groundnut oil, for frying

TO GARNISH
Slices of fresh mango and pineapple
   and fresh chopped coriander

TO SERVE
Glutinous (short-grain) rice, Sweet & Sour
   Sauce *(see page 97)*, fresh chopped
   pineapple, fresh chopped green and
   red peppers and mango chutney

PORK & PEANUT FONDUE

USE EITHER SMOOTH OR CRUNCHY PEANUT BUTTER TO MARINATE THE PORK; THE CHOICE IS YOURS.
WARMING THE PEANUT BUTTER FIRST MAKES IT EASIER TO BLEND WITH THE OTHER INGREDIENTS.

Cut the pork fillet into thin strips and place in a shallow dish. Blend the peanut butter with the chilli, garlic, sugar, soy sauce, lemon juice and groundnut oil. Pour over the pork, stir, cover and leave to marinate in the fridge for at least 30 minutes.

Heat the oil in the fondue pot, then carefully place over the lighted spirit stove.

Drain the pork, thread on to skewers and cook in the hot oil for 3 to 4 minutes or until cooked. Garnish with the lime or lemon wedges and chopped coriander and serve with the Satay Sauce and salad.

Serves **4**
Preparation time **8 to 10 minutes plus 30 minutes marinating time**
Cooking time **3 to 4 minutes per strip**

450 g/1 lb pork fillet
4 Tbsp peanut butter
1 red serrano chilli, deseeded and chopped
2 to 3 garlic cloves, peeled and crushed
2 tsp dark granulated brown sugar
1 Tbsp soy sauce
2 Tbsp lemon juice
2 Tbsp groundnut oil
600 ml/1 pt oil, for frying

TO GARNISH
Lime or lemon wedges, and chopped coriander

TO SERVE
Satay Sauce *(see page 99)* and Mixed Chinese Green Salad *(see page 108)*

APPLE PORK FONDUE

CALVADOS APPLE BRANDY COMES FROM NORMANDY, FRANCE, AND HAS A VERY DISTINCTIVE FLAVOUR. IT IS WELL WORTH BUYING IF YOU GET THE OPPORTUNITY. IF IT IS NOT AVAILABLE, SUBSTITUTE ANOTHER GOOD-QUALITY BRANDY.

Cut the pork into cubes and place in a shallow dish. Scatter over the spring onions, pepper and sage, then mix together the Calvados and apple juice and pour over the pork. Stir lightly, cover and leave to marinate in the fridge for at least 30 minutes. Stir occasionally.

Heat the oil in the fondue pot and carefully place over the lighted spirit stove. Drain the pork and spear with fondue forks.

Cook in the hot oil for 2 to 5 minutes or until cooked. Garnish with the apple wedges and serve with the pasta, sage with black pepper, mayonnaise, salad and bread.

Serves **4 to 6**
Preparation time **5 to 7 minutes plus**
   30 minutes marinating time
Cooking time **2 to 5 minutes per cube**

550 g/1¼ lb pork tenderloin
6 spring onions, trimmed and chopped
Freshly ground black pepper
2 Tbsp chopped fresh sage
3 Tbsp Calvados
120 ml/4 fl oz apple juice
600 ml/1 pt oil, for frying

TO GARNISH
Apple wedges

TO SERVE
Fresh cooked tagliatelle tossed in butter, chopped sage with black pepper, Creamy Herb Mayonnaise *(see page 104)*, **Tossed Green Salad** *(see page 114)* **and crusty bread**

POULTRY

MONGOLIAN CHICKEN HOT POT

THESE HOT POT FONDUES ARE ALSO KNOWN AS ASIAN FONDUES. THE POTS ARE SOMETIMES REFERRED TO AS CHRYSANTHEMUM POTS, DUE TO THE DECORATIVE PATTERN ON THE BASE AND THE WAY THE FLAMES FROM THE SPIRIT STOVE CREATE A WONDERFUL PATTERN IN THE SHAPE OF A CHRYSANTHEMUM.

Cut the chicken into thin strips and place in shallow dishes, cover lightly and store in the fridge until required.

Place the stock in the Mongolian hot pot or fondue pot. Add the chillies, root ginger, garlic, shallots, star anise and honey. Bring to the boil, then simmer for 10 minutes. Place over the lighted spirit stove.

Meanwhile, cut the courgettes into thin strips. Deseed the peppers and cut into thin strips. Place the courgettes and peppers in boiling water for 5 minutes, then drain. Arrange on serving dishes. Garnish with the coriander.

Mix the ingredients for the dipping sauce together and pour into small bowls.

Spear the chicken and the vegetable strips on to the forks and cook in the hot stock for 2 to 4 minutes. When all the chicken and vegetables have been cooked, add the bean sprouts to the stock. Heat for 2 minutes and serve the stock as a soup, garnished with the chopped red chillies.

Serves **6 to 8**
Preparation time **15 minutes**
Cooking time **2 to 4 minutes**
  per strip

900 g/2 lb chicken breast
600 ml/1 pt chicken stock
2 bird's-eye chillies, deseeded
  and crushed
1 Tbsp grated fresh root ginger
3 to 4 garlic cloves, peeled and
  crushed
4 shallots, peeled and chopped
4 star anise
2 to 3 tsp clear honey
2 medium courgettes
1 red pepper
1 yellow pepper
50 g/2 oz bean sprouts

FOR THE DIPPING SAUCE
3 Tbsp light soy sauce
1 tsp clear honey
½ tsp crushed dried chillies
2 tsp dry sherry

TO GARNISH
Chopped coriander and chopped
  red chillies

CHICKEN & CHILLI MEATBALL FONDUE

THIS RECIPE CALLS FOR TOASTED CUMIN SEEDS, WHICH CAN BE DONE IN THREE WAYS: PLACE ON A BAKING SHEET AND COOK IN A HOT OVEN FOR ABOUT 10 MINUTES, SHAKING THE TRAY OCCASIONALLY; OR PLACE ON A FOIL-LINED GRILL PAN AND GRILL UNDER A MODERATE HEAT FOR 2 TO 3 MINUTES; OR SPRINKLE IN A FRYING PAN AND HEAT GENTLY, STIRRING FOR 2 TO 3 MINUTES. TAKE CARE NOT TO BURN THE SEEDS AS THIS WILL IMPAIR THE FLAVOUR.

Serves **4**

Preparation time **15 to 20 minutes including**
  toasting the cumin seeds

Cooking time **3 to 4 minutes per piece**

450 g/1 lb minced chicken

2 to 3 jalapeño chillies, deseeded and chopped

1 tsp toasted cumin seeds

1 small onion, peeled and chopped

2 to 3 garlic cloves, crushed

Salt and freshly ground black pepper

2 Tbsp chopped fresh thyme

600 ml/1 pt oil, for frying

TO GARNISH

Sprigs of thyme

TO SERVE

Green Mayonnaise *(see page 96)*, Indian-style
  Raita *(see page 104)*, Artichoke & Bean
  Salad with Vinaigrette *(see page 110)*
  and crusty bread

Mix together the minced chicken with the chillies, cumin seeds, onion, garlic, seasoning and thyme. Form into small balls. Place in a serving bowl and garnish with the thyme. Cover lightly and chill.

Heat the oil in the fondue pot to 190°C/350°F, then carefully transfer to the lighted spirit stove.

Spear the meatballs on to the fondue fork and cook in the hot oil for 3 to 4 minutes.

Serve with the Green Mayonnaise, Indian-style Raita, Artichoke & Bean Salad with Vinaigrette and bread.

SMOKY CHICKEN FONDUE

A VARIETY OF DRIED CHILLIES IS AVAILABLE, VARYING FROM AROMATIC, SMOKY FLAVOURS TO FRUITY. FOR THIS FONDUE, I WOULD RECOMMEND USING MULATOS OR CHIPOTLES.

Serves **4 to 6**

Preparation time **18 minutes,**
  plus 30 minutes marinating time

Cooking time **2 to 4 minutes per cube**

1 to 2 dried chillies

550 g/1¼ lb boneless chicken breast

4 to 5 whole cloves

1 tsp ground cinnamon

2 Tbsp white wine vinegar

1 Tbsp tomato purée

1 Tbsp Worcestershire sauce

600 ml/1 pt oil, for frying

TO GARNISH

Pickled chillies and coriander sprigs

TO SERVE

Green Tomatillo Sauce *(see page 100)*,
  Soured Cream Sauce *(see page 103)*,
  Spiced Rice Salad *(see page 109)*
  and crusty bread

Dry fry the chillies in a frying pan for 2 to 3 minutes, remove from the heat and place in a small bowl. Cover with 250 ml/8 fl oz very hot (but not boiling) water and leave for at least 10 minutes. Drain the chillies, reserving the liquor and chop finely.

Cut the chicken into cubes and sprinkle the chillies, cloves and cinnamon over the cubes. Blend the vinegar with the tomato purée, Worcestershire sauce and chilli soaking liquor, then pour over the chicken.

Cover lightly, then leave to marinate in the fridge for at least 30 minutes. Stir occasionally during marinating. Heat the oil in the fondue pot to 190°C/350°F and carefully place over the lighted spirit stove.

Drain the chicken, arrange in small bowls, and garnish with pickled chillies and coriander sprigs. Thread the chicken on to the fondue forks and cook in the hot oil for 2 to 4 minutes. Serve with the Green Tomatillo Sauce, Soured Cream Sauce, Spiced Rice Salad and bread.

SOUTHERN CHICKEN FONDUE

THESE TENDER, SUCCULENT STRIPS OF CHICKEN ARE COATED
IN A LIGHT BATTER THEN QUICKLY FRIED.

Serves **4 to 6**
Preparation time **10 minutes plus**
  30 minutes marinating time
Cooking time **3 to 4 minutes per strip**

550 g/1¼ lb chicken breast, cut into strips
4 Tbsp orange juice
1 red serrano chilli, deseeded and crushed
2 to 3 garlic cloves, peeled and crushed
2 Tbsp chopped fresh parsley

FOR THE BATTER
100 g/4 oz plain flour
2 Tbsp cornmeal

½ tsp black pepper
1 tsp hot paprika
1 medium egg, beaten
175 ml/6 fl oz milk
600 ml/1 pt oil, for frying

TO GARNISH
Parsley sprigs and wedges
  of tomato

TO SERVE
Sweetcorn relish and corn bread

Place the chicken in a shallow dish. Mix the orange juice, chilli, garlic and
parsley together and pour over the chicken. Stir, cover lightly and chill for at
least 30 minutes.

Meanwhile, make the batter by sifting the flours into a mixing bowl, then stir in
the peppers. Make a well in the centre and add the egg. Gradually add the milk,
drawing the flour in from the sides of the bowl to form a smooth batter. Leave to
stand for 30 minutes, then stir well just before using.

Heat the oil to 190°C/350°F in the fondue pot and carefully place over the lighted
spirit stove. Place the chicken into serving bowls; and garnish with the parsley
sprigs and tomato wedges.

Thread the chicken on to fondue forks, dip into the batter and cook in the hot oil
for 3 to 4 minutes. Serve with sweetcorn relish and corn bread.

Caribbean Chicken Fondue

CARIBBEAN CHICKEN FONDUE

THESE DAYS THE AVAILABILITY OF MANY DIVERSE FOODS MAKES IT EASY FOR US TO ENJOY THE BEST OF ALL CUISINES, AS CAN BE SEEN IN THIS RECIPE FROM THE SUNNY CARIBBEAN.

Serves **6**
Preparation time **5 to 7 minutes**
   plus 30 minutes marinating time
Cooking time **2 to 4 minutes per piece**

900 g/2 lb chicken breast, cut into cubes
2 Tbsp brown sugar
1 to 3 Scotch bonnet chillies, deseeded and
   finely chopped
3 to 4 garlic cloves, peeled and crushed
2 Tbsp chopped fresh coriander
250 ml/8 fl oz mango juice
600 ml/1 pt oil, for frying

TO GARNISH
Mango wedges and pickled chillies

TO SERVE
Green Tomatillo Sauce *(see page 100)*, **Artichoke Heart Salad** *(see page 115)* **and cooked rice or corn bread**

Place the chicken in a shallow dish. Sprinkle with the sugar, chillies, garlic, and coriander, then pour over the mango juice. Stir lightly, then cover and leave to marinate in the fridge for at least 30 minutes. Stir occasionally.

Heat the oil in the fondue pot to 190°C/350°F then carefully place over the lighted spirit stove.

Drain the chicken, boil the marinade vigorously for 10 minutes or until reduced by half, then pour into small bowls and use as a dipping sauce.

Place the chicken in small bowls and garnish with the mango wedges and pickled chillies.

Spear the chicken on to the fondue forks then cook in the hot oil for 2 to 4 minutes or until cooked. Serve with the Green Tomatillo Sauce, Artichoke Heart Salad and cooked rice or corn bread.

SIZZLING TURKEY FONDUE

THIS FONDUE IS BASED ON THE EVER-POPULAR MEXICAN SIZZLING
FAJITAS. BE SURE THE TURKEY IS WELL COOKED.

Serves **4**
Preparation time **8 to 10 minutes plus
    30 minutes marinating time**
Cooking time **2 to 4 minutes per piece**

550 g/1¼ lb turkey breast, cut into strips
2 to 3 serrano chillies, deseeded and
    chopped or ½ to 1 tsp crushed dried
    chillies
6 spring onions, chopped
3 to 4 garlic cloves, crushed
2 Tbsp chopped fresh coriander
2 tsp warmed clear honey

3 Tbsp lime juice
6 Tbsp olive oil
600 ml/1 pt oil, for frying

TO GARNISH
Lime wedges

TO SERVE
Guacamole, Salsa *(see page 99)*,
    Soured Cream Sauce *(see page
    103)*, shredded spring onions and
    warmed tortilla pancakes

Place the turkey strips in a shallow dish. Scatter over the chillies, spring
onions, garlic and coriander. Mix together the honey, lime juice and olive oil,
and pour over the turkey. Stir, cover and marinate in the fridge for at least
30 minutes.

Heat the oil to 190°C/375°F in the fondue pot then carefully transfer to the
lighted spirit stove.

Drain the turkey, arrange on serving plates and garnish with the lime. Spear
the turkey on to the fondue forks and cook in the hot oil for 2 to 4 minutes.

Serve with the guacamole, Salsa, Soured Cream Sauce, spring onions and
tortilla pancakes.

Sizzling Turkey Fondue

PACIFIC RIM FONDUE

HERE I HAVE COMBINED EASTERN FLAVORS WITH A WESTERN COOKING METHOD—THE RESULT IS DELICIOUS!

Serves **6 to 8**
Preparation time **10 minutes plus 30 minutes marinating time**
Cooking time **2 to 4 minutes per cube**

900 g/2 lb chicken breast, cut into cubes
1 Tbsp grated lime zest
2 bird's-eye chillies, deseeded and chopped
3 garlic cloves, peeled and crushed
2 Tbsp grated fresh root ginger
6 spring onions, chopped
2 Tbsp chopped fresh coriander
4 Tbsp lime juice

3 Tbsp olive oil
1 Tbsp sesame oil
600 ml/1 pt oil, for frying

TO GARNISH
Spring onions and coriander sprigs

TO SERVE
Sweet & Sour Sauce *(see page 97)*, Spicy Pepper & Mushroom Salad *(see page 116)* and Creamy Potato & Apple Salad *(see page 117)*

Place the chicken in a shallow dish. Scatter over the lime zest, chillies, garlic, root ginger, spring onions and coriander. Blend the lime juice with the oils and pour over the chicken. Stir, then cover and chill for at least 30 minutes.

Drain the chicken and place in small bowls, garnished with the spring onions and coriander.

Heat the oil in the fondue pot to 190°C/350°F then place over the lighted spirit stove. Spear the chicken on to the fondue forks and cook in the hot oil for 2 to 4 minutes or until cooked.

Serve with Sweet & Sour Sauce, Spicy Pepper & Mushroom Salad and Creamy Potato & Apple Salad.

HOT 'N' SPICY TURKEY FONDUE

MAKE THIS DISH AS HOT AND FIERY AS YOU DARE, SIMPLY BY INCREASING THE NUMBER OR VARIETY OF CHILLIES USED, AND—FOR THE REALLY BRAVE—KEEPING THE SEEDS AND MEMBRANE IN THE CHILLIES.

Cut the turkey into strips and place in a shallow dish. Mix together the chillies, garlic, Tabasco Sauce, coriander, honey, lime juice and the 6 tablespoons oil, and pour over the turkey. Cover and leave to marinate in the fridge for at least 30 minutes. Drain and arrange in small bowls, and garnish with coriander sprigs, pickled chillies and tomato wedges.

Heat the pint of oil to 190°C/375°F in the fondue pot and carefully place on the lighted spirit stove. Thread the turkey strips on to the fondue forks or skewers and cook in the hot oil for 2 to 4 minutes.

Serve with the tortilla pancakes, lettuce, spring onions, Salsa and Soured Cream Sauce.

Serves **6 to 8**
Preparation time **8 to 10 minutes plus 30 minutes marinating time**
Cooking time **2 to 4 minutes per strip**

900 g/2 lb turkey breast
2 to 3 chillies, deseeded and chopped
3 to 4 garlic cloves, peeled and chopped
2 to 3 tsp Tabasco Sauce
2 Tbsp chopped fresh coriander
2 tsp warmed clear honey
3 Tbsp lime juice
6 Tbsp oil
600 ml/1 pt oil, for frying

TO GARNISH
Coriander sprigs, pickled chillies, tomato wedges

TO SERVE
Warmed tortilla pancakes, shredded lettuce, shredded spring onions, Salsa *(see page 99)* and Soured Cream Sauce *(see page 103)*

TURKEY & SATAY FONDUE

IF YOU ARE WEIGHT-CONSCIOUS, THIS FONDUE IS IDEAL, AS TURKEY IS VERY LOW IN FAT—LOWER IN FAT THAN CHICKEN. THE TURKEY IS MARINATED IN LOW-FAT YOGURT AND QUICKLY FRIED AND DRAINED.

Cut the turkey breast into strips and place in a shallow dish. Blend together the yoghurt, peanut butter, orange zest and juice, chilli and grated root ginger. Pour over the turkey and stir. Cover and leave to marinate in the fridge for at least 30 minutes. Stir occasionally during marinating.

Heat the oil to 190°C/375°F in the fondue pot and carefully place on the lighted spirit stove.

Thread the turkey on to the fondue forks and cook in the hot oil for 2 to 4 minutes. Drain on kitchen paper if preferred. Garnish with the orange wedges, flat-leaf parsley and chilli, and serve with the Satay Sauce, Spiced Rice Salad and bread.

Serves **4 to 6**
Preparation time **10 minutes plus 30 minutes marinating time**
Cooking time **2 to 4 minutes per strip**

550 g/1¼ lb turkey breast
6 Tbsp low-fat, natural yoghurt
3 Tbsp smooth or crunchy peanut butter, warmed
2 Tbsp grated orange zest
4 Tbsp orange juice
1 bird's-eye chilli, deseeded and chopped
1 Tbsp grated fresh root ginger
600 ml/1 pt oil, for frying

TO GARNISH
Orange wedges, flat-leaf parsley and chopped red chilli

TO SERVE
Satay Sauce (see page 99), **Spiced Rice Salad** (see page 109), **and crusty bread**

CRISPY TURKEY FONDUE

LITTLE MORSELS OF TURKEY, DELICATELY FLAVOURED WITH MINT AND LEMON, WILL MAKE THIS FONDUE POPULAR WITH EVERYONE.

Mix together the minced turkey, chopped mint, lemon zest, onion and garlic, with seasoning to taste. Form into small balls.

Place the beaten egg into a shallow dish and the breadcrumbs in a separate dish. Dip the turkey balls in the egg, allowing any excess to drip back into the bowl, then coat in the breadcrumbs. Arrange on serving plates and garnish with lemon wedges and mint sprigs. Chill, lightly covered, until required.

Heat the oil in the fondue pot to 190°C/350°F, then carefully transfer to the lighted spirit stove. Cook the turkey balls in the oil for 3 to 5 minutes, or until they are cooked.

Serve with the Sweet & Sour Sauce, Chilled Ratatouille, Zesty Orange Coleslaw and new potatoes.

Serves **4 to 6**
Preparation time **10 minutes**
Cooking time **3 to 5 minutes per piece**

450 g/1 lb fresh minced turkey
2 Tbsp chopped fresh mint
2 Tbsp grated lemon zest
1 small onion, peeled and grated
2 to 3 garlic cloves, peeled and crushed
Salt and freshly ground black pepper
1 medium egg, beaten
175 g/6 oz dried breadcrumbs
600 ml/1 pt oil, for frying

TO GARNISH
Lemon wedges and mint sprigs.

TO SERVE
Sweet & Sour Sauce *(see page 97)*,
  Chilled Ratatouille *(see page 109)*,
  Zesty Orange Coleslaw *(see page 114)*
  and freshly cooked new potatoes

LEMON TURKEY FONDUE

MARINATING THE TURKEY IN THE LEMON JUICE AND CORNFLOUR MAKES IT MELT IN THE MOUTH. TRY FOR YOURSELF AND SEE.

Cut the turkey into cubes and place in a shallow dish. Mix together the lemon zest and juice, olive oil, cornflour, chillies and soy sauce. Pour over the turkey and stir lightly. Cover and leave to marinate in the fridge for at least 30 minutes. Stir occasionally during marinating.

Drain the turkey, place in serving bowls and garnish with the lemon wedges and parsley sprigs.

Heat the oil to 190°C/350°F in the fondue pot and carefully place over a lighted spirit stove. Spear the turkey cubes with fondue forks and cook in the hot oil for 2 to 4 minutes, or until cooked.

Serve with the Blue Cheese Dressing, Green Mayonnaise, Tossed Green Salad and glutinous rice.

Serves **6 to 8**
Preparation time **8 minutes plus 30 minutes marinating time**
Cooking time **2 to 4 minutes per cube**

900 g/2 lb turkey breast
2 Tbsp grated lemon zest
6 Tbsp lemon juice
2 Tbsp olive oil
3 Tbsp cornflour
1 to 2 tsp crushed dried chillies
2 Tbsp light soy sauce
600 ml/1 pt oil, for frying

TO GARNISH
Lemon wedges and flat-leaf parsley sprigs

TO SERVE
Blue Cheese Dressing *(see page 96)*, **Green Mayonnaise** *(see page 96)*, **Tossed Green Salad** *(see page 114)* **and cooked glutinous (short-grain) rice**

MARINATED DUCK FONDUE

IF POSSIBLE, USE BARBARY DUCK FOR THIS RECIPE. THE BREASTS ARE PLUMP AND FULL
OF FLAVOUR, WHICH IS SEALED IN BY COOKING QUICKLY IN HOT OIL.

Remove the skin and any fat from the duck. Cut into thin strips, and place in a shallow dish.

Gently warm the marmalade, then stir in the orange juice, sage and walnut oil. Pour over the duck breast, stir, then cover and leave to marinate in the fridge for at least 30 minutes. Stir occasionally during marinating.

Heat the oil in the fondue pot to 190°C/350°F, and carefully place over the lighted spirit stove.

Drain the duck and place in a serving bowl. Garnish with the strips of orange peel and sage leaves.

Spear the duck strips on to the fondue forks or skewers and cook in the hot oil for 2 to 4 minutes or until cooked.

Serve with the Sweet & Sour Sauce, Orange Cumberland Dipping Sauce, Artichoke Heart Salad and new potatoes.

Serves **4**
Preparation time **10 minutes plus
  30 minutes marinating time**
Cooking time **2 to 4 minutes per strip**

3 to 4 duck breasts, depending on size
4 Tbsp orange marmalade
3 Tbsp orange juice
2 Tbsp chopped fresh sage
2 Tbsp walnut oil
600 ml/1 pt oil, for frying

TO GARNISH
Fine strips of orange peel and sage leaves

TO SERVE
Sweet & Sour Sauce *(see page 97)*,
  Orange Cumberland Dipping Sauce
  (see page 102), **Artichoke Heart Salad**
  (see page 115) **and freshly cooked
  new potatoes**

RED DUCK FONDUE

LIKE STEAK, DUCK BREAST CAN BE EATEN EITHER RARE OR WELL DONE.

Serves **4**
Preparation time **10 minutes** plus 30 minutes marinating time
Cooking time **2 to 4 minutes** per piece

3 to 4 duck breasts, according to size
4 Tbsp plum jam
2 Tbsp lemon juice
1 tsp dried crushed chillies
1 Tbsp granulated dark brown sugar
1 Tbsp soy sauce
600 ml/1 pt oil, for frying

TO GARNISH
Ripe plum slices and flat-leaf parsley sprigs

TO SERVE
Orange Cumberland Dipping Sauce *(see page 102)*, Spiced Rice Salad *(see page 109)* and Artichoke & Bean Salad with Vinaigrette *(see page 110)*

Discard the skin and fat from the duck breasts and cut into thin strips. Place in a shallow dish.

Warm the jam, then stir in the lemon juice, chillies, sugar and soy sauce. Pour over the duck breasts, stir well, cover and leave to marinate in the fridge for at least 30 minutes. Stir occasionally during marinating.

Heat the oil in the fondue pot to 190°C/350°F, then carefully place over the lighted spirit stove.

Drain the duck and spear on to fondue forks or skewers. Cook in the hot oil for 2 to 4 minutes .

Garnish with the plum slices and parsley, and serve with Orange Cumberland Dipping Sauce, Spiced Rice Salad and Artichoke & Bean Salad with Vinaigrette.

DUCK & TOMATILLOS FONDUE

TOMATILLOS CAN BE BOUGHT FRESH OR CANNED.

Serves **4**
Preparation time **10 to 12 minutes** plus 30 minutes marinating time
Cooking time **2 to 4 minutes** per cube

3 to 4 duck breasts, depending on size
225 g/8 oz tomatillos or green tomatoes, deseeded and chopped
2 Fresno chillies, deseeded and chopped
1 small onion, chopped
2 to 3 garlic cloves, crushed
1 Tbsp grated lemon zest, optional
2 Tbsp chopped fresh coriander
5 Tbsp olive oil
2 Tbsp balsamic vinegar
600 ml/1 pt oil, for frying

TO GARNISH
Coriander sprigs and lemon wedges

TO SERVE
Salsa *(see page 99)*, Spicy Pepper & Mushroom Salad *(see page 116)* and warm tortilla pancakes

Skin the duck breasts, cut into cubes, and place in a shallow dish. Place the chopped tomatillos or tomatoes in a food processor with the chillies, onion, garlic and lemon zest if using. Blend to a purée. Stir in the coriander, olive oil and balsamic vinegar, then pour over the duck. Stir until coated. Cover, and leave to marinate in the fridge for at least 30 minutes. Stir occasionally.

Heat the oil to 190°C/350°F in the fondue pot, and carefully place over the lighted spirit stove. Drain the duck and spear with fondue forks or skewers. Cook in the hot oil for 2 to 4 minutes.

Garnish with coriander and lemon wedges, and serve with the Salsa, Spicy Pepper & Mushroom Salad and tortilla pancakes.

CHEESE

TRADITIONAL SWISS FONDUE

REPUTED TO BE THE ORIGINAL OF ALL CHEESE FONDUES, THIS IS NOW THE NATIONAL DISH OF SWITZERLAND. MAKE SURE YOU BUY GENUINE SWISS GRUYÈRE AND EMMENTAL CHEESE, AS THEY ARE LESS LIKELY TO "LUMP" THAN OTHER VARIETIES.

Cut the garlic clove, then rub it around the inside of the fondue pot. Pour in the wine and lemon juice, and place over the lighted spirit stove. Gradually add the cheeses, stirring throughout until completely melted.

When the cheese has melted and begins to bubble, blend the cornflour with the kirsch and stir into the pot. Cook, stirring, for 2 to 3 minutes. Add remaining ingredients to taste, then serve with the Tossed Green Salad, cubes of French bread to dip into the fondue and pear slices to freshen the palate.

Serves **4**
Preparation time **10 minutes**
Cooking time **10 to 12 minutes**

1 garlic clove
150 ml/¼ pt dry white wine
Squeeze of lemon juice
225 g/8 oz Gruyère cheese, grated
225 g/8 oz Emmental cheese, grated
1 Tbsp cornflour

2 Tbsp kirsch
Pinch of salt
¼ tsp paprika
¼ tsp grated nutmeg

TO SERVE

Tossed Green Salad *(see page 114)*, **cubes of French bread for dipping and fresh ripe pear slices**

BRIE & LOBSTER FONDUE

THIS FONDUE IS DEFINITELY ONE FOR WHEN YOU ARE OUT TO IMPRESS. IT IS WICKEDLY CREAMY AND FOR EVEN GREATER ENJOYMENT YOU CAN SERVE IT WITH FRESHLY COOKED SCALLOPS, DUBLIN BAY PRAWNS, ASPARAGUS SPEARS, BREADSTICKS AND PRETZELS.

Melt the butter in the fondue pot and gently sauté the shallots for 10 minutes, or until softened but not coloured. Sprinkle in the flour and cook for a further 2 minutes.

Gradually add the stock, stirring throughout until the mixture thickens, then simmer for 4 minutes.

Discard any unwanted rind from the Brie and cut into cubes. Stir into the fondue with the cream. Continue to cook, stirring until the mixture is smooth.

Stir in the flaked lobster meat with the lemon juice, Tabasco Sauce, black pepper and paprika, and heat through.

Carefully place over the lighted spirit stove, stir in the chopped parsley and serve with the dippers and salads.

Serves **4**
Preparation time **10 minutes**
Cooking time **22 to 25 minutes**

25 g/1 oz butter
4 shallots, peeled and chopped
2 Tbsp plain flour
350 ml/12 fl oz fish or chicken stock
350 g/12 oz ripe French Brie
150 ml/¼ pt double cream
225 g/8 oz cooked lobster meat,
**   flaked**
2 Tbsp lemon juice
Tabasco Sauce to taste
Freshly ground black pepper
1 tsp paprika
1 Tbsp chopped fresh parsley

TO SERVE

Freshly cooked scallops, Dublin Bay
**   prawns, blanched asparagus**
**   spears, breadsticks and pretzels**
**   for dipping. Tossed Green Salad**
**   (see page 114) and Artichoke Heart**
**   Salad (see page 115)**

DEVILLED CRAB & CHEESE FONDUE

USE FRESH CRAB MEAT IF YOU CAN, AS THE FLAVOUR IS FAR SUPERIOR TO THAT OF CANNED OR FROZEN. IF FRESH CRAB MEAT IS NOT AVAILABLE, USE A LITTLE EXTRA TABASCO SAUCE TO HELP DEVELOP THE FLAVOUR OF THE FONDUE.

Serves **4**
Preparation time **8 to 10 minutes**
Cooking time **7 to 9 minutes**

150 ml/¼ pt dry white wine
350 g/12 oz Gruyère cheese, grated
100 g/4 oz Roquefort cheese, crumbled
50 g/2 oz Boursin Natural cheese
1 Tbsp cornflour
1 tsp dry mustard powder
225 g/8 oz white crab meat, flaked
¼ to ½ tsp Tabasco Sauce
1 Tbsp lemon juice
4 spring onions, chopped

TO SERVE
Crusty bread, cooked large prawns, wedges of cucumber and chicory leaves for dipping, and Artichoke & Bean Salad with Vinaigrette *(see page 110)*

Pour the wine into the fondue pot and heat gently, then carefully place over the lighted spirit stove.

Toss the cheeses in the cornflour and add the mustard powder. Gradually add to the wine, stirring continuously. When all the cheese has been added, stir in the crab meat with the Tabasco Sauce, lemon juice and spring onions. Heat gently, stirring throughout until thick, then serve with the dippers and salad.

CALIFORNIAN FONDUE

HERE I HAVE USED A ROSÉ WINE FROM THE NAPA VALLEY. LOOK FOR ONE THAT IS ON THE DRY SIDE RATHER THAN SWEET. THE USE OF ROSÉ WINE GIVES THE FONDUE A WONDERFUL ROSY COLOUR, BEAUTIFULLY OFFSET BY THE PINK OF THE PRAWNS.

Serves **4**
Preparation time **10 minutes**
Cooking time **10 minutes**

1 garlic clove
150 ml/¼ pt rosé wine
350 g/12 oz Gruyère cheese, grated
1 Tbsp cornflour
1 Tbsp kirsch
100 g/4 oz soured cream
¼ tsp grated nutmeg
Freshly ground black pepper
100 g/4 oz cooked prawns, peeled and chopped
2 Tbsp freshly snipped chives

TO SERVE
Natural cubes of challah bread, wedges of pineapple, melon, ripe pears and apples for dipping. Zesty Orange Coleslaw *(see page 114)* **and Spicy Pepper & Mushroom Salad** *(see page 116)*

Cut the garlic and rub on the insides of the fondue pot. Pour in the wine and heat gently. Place over the lighted spirit stove.

Toss the cheese in the cornflour then gradually add to the wine and heat gently, stirring continuously until melted.

Stir in the kirsch, soured cream, nutmeg and black pepper to taste. Continue to cook until thickened, then stir in the chopped prawns and the chives. Heat through for 2 to 3 minutes before serving with the dippers and salads.

STILTON FONDUE

STILTON IS A STRONG CHEESE AND THEREFORE NEEDS THE STRONG FLAVOURS OF LAGER, MUSTARD AND PAPRIKA TO ACCOMPANY IT. FOR SOMETHING A LITTLE DIFFERENT, SERVE THE STILTON WITH FRESH OR READY-TO-EAT DRIED APRICOTS.

Heat the lager in the fondue pot then carefully place over the lighted spirit stove.

Toss the cheeses in the cornflour and gradually stir into the lager, stirring continuously. When all the cheese has been added, stir in the mustard and paprika, and continue to heat gently until thick and creamy.

Serve with the dippers and salads.

Serves **4**
Preparation time **10 minutes**
Cooking time **10 minutes**

225 g/8 fl oz lager
350 g/12 oz blue Stilton cheese,
   crumbled
100 g/4 oz Monterey Jack cheese, grated
2 Tbsp cornflour
1 tsp wholegrain mustard
1 tsp hot paprika

TO SERVE
Baby button mushrooms, apple wedges,
   large red Flame Tokay and seedless
   white grapes and wedges of melon for
   dipping. Chunks of blue Stilton,
   Mediterranean Salad *(see page 112)*
   and Spicy Pepper & Mushroom Salad
   (see page 116)

SMOKY BACON & CHEESE FONDUE

THE INFORMALITY OF A FONDUE PARTY MEANS IT IS AN IDEAL WAY OF INTRODUCING PEOPLE TO EACH OTHER. CONVERSATION FLOWS FREELY WHILE EVERYONE DIPS INTO THE FONDUE POT. FONDUE PARTIES ARE ALSO EASY ON THE HOSTS, AS THEY CAN JOIN IN AND NOT BE FOREVER CHECKING ON THE FOOD.

Heat the butter in a small pan and sauté the garlic and shallots for 5 minutes, or until softened. Add the bacon and continue to sauté gently for 5 to 8 minutes or until the bacon is crisp. Drain on kitchen paper.

Heat the wine in the fondue pan, then place over the lighted spirit stove. Toss the cheeses in the cornflour then gradually stir into the wine, stirring continuously. Once the cheese has melted, stir in the drained bacon and shallots, paprika, chilli sauce and parsley. Heat until thick, then serve with the dippers, bread and Zesty Orange Coleslaw.

Serves **8**
Preparation time **15 minutes**
Cooking time **20 to 23 minutes**

1 Tbsp butter

1 to 2 garlic cloves, peeled and crushed

4 shallots, peeled and chopped

225 g/8 oz smoked bacon rashers, chopped

250 ml/8 fl oz dry white wine

450 g/1 lb Gruyère cheese, grated

225 g/8 oz Monterey Jack cheese, grated

2 Tbsp cornflour

1 tsp paprika

¼ to ½ tsp chilli sauce, or to taste

1 Tbsp chopped fresh parsley

TO SERVE

Wedges of apple and fresh pineapple, celery and carrot sticks, cubes of crusty bread for dipping and Zesty Orange Coleslaw *(see page 114)*

AUTUMN FONDUE

DON'T BE DECEIVED BY ITS NAME, THIS FONDUE IS GOOD ENOUGH TO EAT ALL YEAR ROUND.

Serves **6 to 8**
Preparation time **12 minutes**
Cooking time **12 to 14 minutes**

1 garlic clove
150 ml/¼ pt dry white wine
150 ml/¼ pt cranberry-apple juice
350 g/12 oz Emmental cheese, grated
225 g/8 oz Monterey Jack cheese, grated
2 Tbsp cornflour
1 tsp dry mustard powder
2 Tbsp Calvados or other brandy

TO SERVE
Cubes of wholemeal bread, strips of yellow and red bell pepper, carrot and celery sticks, apple wedges, broccoli florets, freshly cooked potatoes, Avocado & Mango Salad *(see page 106)* and Chilled Ratatouille *(see page 109)*

Cut the garlic and rub it on the insides of the fondue pot. Pour in the wine and cranberry and apple juice. Heat gently, then place over the lighted spirit stove.

Toss the cheeses in the cornflour and mustard powder, then gradually stir into the wine. Cook, stirring continuously, until the cheese has melted.

Stir in the Calvados or other brandy and continue to cook until thick and creamy. Serve with the dippers, potatoes and salads.

BRANDY & WALNUT FONDUE

THE FLAVOUR OF THE WALNUTS IS HEIGHTENED BY THE CALVADOS BRANDY AND CHEESE USED IN THIS FONDUE. IF CALVADOS IS UNAVAILABLE, ANY GOOD BRANDY CAN BE SUBSTITUTED.

Serves **6 to 8**
Preparation time **10 to 12 minutes**
Cooking time **10 minutes**

1 garlic clove
250 ml/8 fl oz dry white wine
4 Tbsp Calvados brandy
225 g/8 oz mature Cheddar cheese, grated
350 g/12 oz Gruyère cheese, grated
100 g/4 oz goat's cheese, crumbled
2 Tbsp cornflour
2 tsp Worcestershire sauce
½ tsp Tabasco Sauce, or to taste
100 g/4 oz chopped walnuts

TO SERVE
Cubes of crusty bread, strips of courgettes, apple and mango wedges, pickled jalapeño chillies for dipping. Chilled Ratatouille *(see page 109)* and Tossed Green Salad *(see page 114)*

Cut the garlic and rub it on the insides of the fondue pot. Pour in the wine and brandy. Heat gently, then place over the lighted spirit stove.

Toss the cheeses in the cornflour then gradually stir into the wine. Heat gently, stirring until all the cheese has melted.

Stir in the Worcestershire sauce, Tabasco Sauce and walnuts. Continue to heat, stirring throughout until thick and creamy. Serve with the dippers and salads.

DUTCH CHEESE FONDUE

WITH A MILD CHEESE SUCH AS GOUDA, IT IS A GOOD IDEA TO ADD SOME MUSTARD AND CAYENNE PEPPER TO DEVELOP THE FLAVOUR OF THE FONDUE.

Cut the garlic clove, then rub it on the insides of the fondue pot. Carefully place the pot over the lighted spirit stove. Pour in the wine and heat gently.

Gradually add the cheese, stirring throughout until the cheese has melted. Mix the mustard powder to a paste with the brandy and 1 tablespoon of water, then stir into the fondue. Add the cayenne pepper to taste.

Blend the cornflour with 2 tablespoons of water and stir into the fondue. Cook for 2 to 3 minutes, stirring throughout until thickened, then serve with the bread and salad vegetables for dipping.

Serves **6**
Preparation time **10 minutes**
Cooking time **10 to 12 minutes**

1 garlic clove
250 ml/8 fl oz dry white wine
450 g/1 lb Gouda cheese, grated
1 to 2 tsp dry mustard powder
1 Tbsp brandy
Cayenne pepper
1½ Tbsp cornflour

TO SERVE

Chunks of warm wholemeal bread, wedges of apple, cucumber, radishes, cherry tomatoes and celery sticks for dipping

RED PEPPER & CHEESE FONDUE

I USUALLY PREFER TO SKIN PEPPERS BEFORE USING AS THIS MAKES THEM MORE DIGESTIBLE (SEE CIDER & RED PEPPER FONDUE, PAGE 84). HOWEVER, FOR DIPPERS, RAW PEPPERS ARE BETTER AS THEY STAY CRISP WHEN DIPPED INTO THE HOT FONDUE.

Pour the cider into the fondue pot and heat gently. Toss the Gruyère cheese in the cornflour then slowly add to the cider, stirring well. When all the Gruyère has been added, stir in the Gorgonzola, pepper, sweetcorn, Tabasco Sauce and pepper to taste. Continue to heat gently, still stirring, until the mixture becomes thick and creamy.

Stir the chopped basil, capers and olives into the fondue pot and gently heat through.

Carefully place the fondue over the lighted spirit stove and serve with the dippers and salads.

Serves **6**
Preparation time **20 minutes including** skinning the pepper
Cooking time **10 minutes**

250 ml/8 fl oz dry cider
350 g/12 oz Gruyère cheese, grated
2 Tbsp cornflour
100 g/4 oz Gorgonzola cheese, crumbled
1 red pepper, deseeded, skinned and chopped
200 g/7 oz tinned creamed sweetcorn
¼ to ½ tsp Tabasco Sauce

Freshly ground black pepper
2 Tbsp chopped fresh basil
1 to 2 Tbsp capers
65 g/2½ oz stoned chopped black olives

TO SERVE

Cooked chipolata sausages, cubes of wholemeal or focaccia bread, red and yellow bell pepper strips, celery and carrot sticks for dipping. Spiced Rice Salad *(see page 109)* and Mediterranean Salad *(see page 112)*

MUSHROOM & ONION FONDUE

DRIED MUSHROOMS ARE READILY AVAILABLE IN MOST STORES. THEY ARE AN IDEAL INGREDIENT TO KEEP IN THE PANTRY AS THEY CAN QUICKLY BE REHYDRATED AND USED IN RISOTTOS, CASSEROLES, OMELETTES AND PASTA DISHES. WHEREVER POSSIBLE, USE THE SOAKING LIQUOR AS IT WILL BE FULL OF FLAVOUR.

Cover the dried mushrooms with very hot (but not boiling) water and leave for 20 minutes. Drain, reserving 120 ml/4 fl oz of the liquor, and finely chop the rehydrated mushrooms.

Heat the oil in the fondue pot and gently sauté the shallots, chilli, and garlic for 5 minutes. Add the chopped button mushrooms and rehydrated mushrooms, and continue to sauté for 3 minutes. Sprinkle in the flour, cook for 2 more minutes, and gradually stir in the reserved soaking liquor, and then the wine and brandy. Carefully place over the lighted spirit stove.

Cook, stirring, until the mixture thickens, then gradually stir in the grated Gruyère. Continue to heat, stirring until the cheese has melted and the mixture is creamy.

Stir in the cream, heat gently, then serve with the dippers and salads.

Serves **6 to 8**
Preparation time **10 minutes plus 20 minutes soaking time**
Cooking time **20 minutes**

2 Tbsp dried mushrooms such as porcini or cèpes
3 Tbsp olive oil
4 shallots, chopped
1 red serrano chilli, deseeded and chopped
2 to 3 garlic cloves, crushed
100 g/4 oz closed-cap button mushrooms, chopped
3 Tbsp plain flour
250 ml/8 fl oz dry white wine
2 Tbsp brandy
450 g/1 lb Gruyère cheese, grated
2 Tbsp single cream

TO SERVE
Chunks of red and yellow pepper, courgette sticks, cherry tomatoes, seedless flame and white grapes, cubes of focaccia bread for dipping. Chilled Ratatouille *(see page 109)*, Tossed Green Salad *(see page 114)* and Red Bean & Pepperoni Salad *(see page 118)*

SAGE FONDUE

IF YOU CANNOT FIND SAGE DERBY CHEESE, INCREASE THE AMOUNT OF GRUYÈRE, AND ADD SOME CHOPPED FRESH SAGE TO THE FONDUE.

Serves **4 to 6**
Preparation time **10 minutes**
Cooking time **10 minutes**

1 garlic clove
450 ml/¾ pt apple juice
350 g/12 oz Gruyère cheese, grated
100 g/4 oz Sage Derby cheese, grated
2 Tbsp cornflour
1 to 2 Tbsp chopped fresh sage
Freshly ground black pepper

TO SERVE
Fresh apple and pear wedges, strips of red and yellow pepper, broccoli and cauliflower florets and cherry tomatoes for dipping, Tossed Green Salad *(see page 114)* and warm chunks of crusty wholemeal bread

Cut the garlic and rub it on the insides of the fondue pot. Pour in the apple juice, and heat gently. Carefully place over the lighted spirit stove.

Toss the cheeses and cornflour together, then gradually stir into the apple juice, stirring throughout until the cheese has melted.

Add the chopped sage and pepper to taste, then stir until thick and creamy. Serve with the dippers, Tossed Green Salad and bread.

LAGER FONDUE

AS ITS NAME SUGGESTS, LAGER OR BEER WOULD BE THE IDEAL DRINK TO SERVE WITH THIS FONDUE.

Serves **4 to 6**
Preparation time **10 minutes**
Cooking time **10 to 12 minutes**

1 garlic clove
250 ml/8 fl oz lager or light ale
225 g/8 oz Monterey Jack cheese, grated
100 g/4 oz Emmental cheese, grated
2 Tbsp cornflour
175 g/6 oz Roquefort cheese, crumbled
¼ to ½ tsp Tabasco Sauce, or to taste
1 tsp Dijon mustard
Freshly ground black pepper

TO SERVE
Pickled jalapeño chillies, large pickled gherkins, large stoned olives and cubes of warm French bread for dipping. Zesty Orange Coleslaw *(see page 114)*, Red Bean & Pepperoni Salad *(see page 118)* and potato skins or wedges

Cut the garlic and rub it on the inside of the fondue pot. Pour in the lager or light ale. Heat gently then carefully place the pot on the lighted spirit stove. Toss the Monterey Jack and Emmental cheeses in the cornflour, then add to the pot. Cook gently, stirring well, until the cheese has melted.

Stir in the Roquefort, Tabasco Sauce, Dijon mustard and freshly ground black pepper to taste. Continue to cook, stirring until the mixture is smooth and creamy. Serve with the dippers, salads and potato skins or wedges.

MANHATTAN FONDUE

I AM PARTICULARLY FOND OF CREAM CHEESE THAT IS FLAVOURED WITH BLACK PEPPER. HOWEVER, IF THIS IS NOT AVAILABLE, LOOK FOR CREAM CHEESE WITH OTHER FLAVOURINGS, SUCH AS HERBS OR CHIVES. LOW-FAT CREAM CHEESE WORKS JUST AS WELL AS FULL-FAT.

Cut the garlic and rub it on the insides of the fondue pot, then pour in the wine. Heat gently, then carefully place over the lighted spirit stove.

Toss the Monterey Jack cheese in the cornflour and gradually add to the wine, stirring throughout. Add the cream cheese and lemon juice. Continue to cook gently, stirring continuously until the mixture has thickened.

Stir in the chopped spring onions, smoked salmon and Tabasco Sauce to taste. Heat gently until thick, then serve with the dippers and salads.

Serves **4 to 6**
Preparation time **7 to 9 minutes**
Cooking time **10 minutes**

1 garlic clove
150 ml/¼ pt dry white wine
300 g/10 oz Monterey Jack cheese, grated
2 tsp cornflour
175 g/6 oz cream cheese with black pepper, cubed
1 Tbsp lemon juice
6 spring onions, chopped
100 g/4 oz smoked salmon, chopped
Tabasco Sauce

TO SERVE
Pretzels, breadsticks and cubed bagels for dipping. Sauerkraut Salad (see page 107) and Artichoke Heart Salad (see page 115)

VIRGINIA FONDUE

MUSTARD HELPS TO BRING OUT THE FLAVOUR OF THE CHEESE. IF WHOLEGRAIN MUSTARD
IS NOT AVAILABLE, ADD A TEASPOON OF MUSTARD POWDER TO THE FLOUR.

Melt the butter in the fondue pot and sprinkle in the flour. Cook
for 2 minutes then stir in the mustard, horseradish and then
the milk. Continue to cook, stirring well until the mixture thickens.

Gradually stir in the grated cheeses, season to taste then add
the sherry.

Continue to cook until the mixture is thick and creamy. Stir in
the chopped ham. Carefully transfer to the lighted spirit stove
and serve with the dippers and salads.

Serves **4 to 6**
Preparation time **10 minutes**
Cooking time **12 to 14 minutes**

50 g/2 oz butter

3 Tbsp plain flour

1 tsp wholegrain mustard

1 tsp creamed horseradish sauce

250 ml/8 fl oz milk

350 g/12 oz Monterey Jack cheese, grated

100 g/4 oz feta cheese, grated or crumbled

Salt and freshly ground black pepper

4 Tbsp dry sherry

175 g/6 oz Virginia ham, chopped

TO SERVE

Celery and carrot sticks, cauliflower
   florets, cherry tomatoes, button
   mushrooms and cubes of rye bread
   for dipping. Sauerkraut Salad *(see
   page 107)*, Spicy Pepper & Mushroom
   Salad *(see page 116)* and Creamy
   Potato & Apple Salad *(see page 117)*

VEGETABLES

CIDER & RED PEPPER FONDUE

PEPPERS TASTE BETTER AND ARE MORE DIGESTIBLE IF THEY ARE SKINNED BEFORE USING IN A COOKED DISH. SIMPLY CUT THE PEPPERS INTO QUARTERS AND PLACE UNDER A PREHEATED GRILL FOR ABOUT 10 MINUTES. SEAL IN A PLASTIC BAG AND LEAVE UNTIL COOL, THEN SKIN.

Melt the butter in the fondue pot and gently sauté the spring onions for 3 minutes. Add the cider to the fondue pot. Heat through, then carefully place over the lighted spirit stove.

Add the grated cheese to the pot and heat, stirring until the cheese has melted.

Add the peppers, sweetcorn and chopped olives, with black pepper to taste, and heat, stirring until thick and creamy. Just before serving, sprinkle in the chopped basil if using, garnish with the baby basil leaves and serve with the dippers, sauce and salads.

Serves **6**
Preparation time **10 to 12 minutes**
Cooking time **11 to 13 minutes**

50 g/2 oz butter
8 spring onions, trimmed and chopped
300 ml/½ pt medium-dry cider
450 g/1 lb Gruyère cheese, grated
2 red peppers, skinned and chopped
175 g/6 oz tinned sweetcorn
65 g/2½ oz stoned black or green olives, chopped
Freshly ground black pepper
1 Tbsp chopped fresh basil, optional

TO GARNISH
Baby basil leaves

TO SERVE
Baby sweetcorn, breadsticks, pretzels, red, yellow and green pepper strips and fresh pear wedges for dipping. Green Tomatillo Sauce *(see page 100)*, **Artichoke Heart Salad** *(see page 115)* **and Mint & Lemon Tabbouleh** *(see page 118)*

APPLE & ARTICHOKE FONDUE

APPLE JUICE COMES BOTH CLEAR AND CLOUDY. I WOULD RECOMMEND THE CLEAR
VARIETY, NOT FOR TASTE BUT FOR APPEARANCE.

Heat the apple juice in the fondue pot and when hot place over
the lighted spirit stove. Stir in the cheeses and continue to
heat, stirring until the cheese has melted. Add the chopped
artichoke hearts and spring onions, then season with pepper.

In a small bowl blend the cornflour with the Calvados and stir
into the fondue. Continue to cook until thickened. Serve with
the mayonnaise, dippers and salads.

Serves **6 to 8**
Preparation time **10 minutes**
Cooking time **15 minutes**

300 ml/½ pt apple juice
350 g/12 oz Emmental cheese, grated
100 g/4 oz goat's cheese, crumbled
175 g/6 oz tinned artichoke hearts, chopped
6 spring onions, chopped
Freshly ground black pepper
2 Tbsp cornflour
3 Tbsp Calvados or other brandy

TO SERVE

Apple wedges, courgette and carrot sticks,
   and crusty bread for dipping. Green
   Mayonnaise *(see page 96)*, Artichoke Heart
   Salad *(see page 115)* and Spicy Pepper &
   Mushroom Salad *(see page 116)*

APPLE & WATERCRESS FONDUE

SORREL WOULD MAKE AN EXCELLENT SUBSTITUTE FOR THE WATERCRESS.

Serves **4 to 6**
Preparation time **10 minutes**
Cooking time **15 minutes**

1 garlic clove
250 ml/8 fl oz apple juice
2 Tbsp brandy
300 g/10 oz Emmental cheese, grated
100 g/4 oz Gorgonzola cheese, crumbled
1 Tbsp cornflour
2 tsp clear honey
Freshly ground black pepper

40 g/1½ oz watercress, chopped

TO SERVE

Watercress sprigs, wedges of apple and pineapple, blanched asparagus spears, pickled onions and cubes of soda or wholemeal bread for dipping. Mint & Lemon Tabbouleh (*see page 118*)

Cut the garlic and rub it on the insides of the fondue pot. Pour in the apple juice and brandy. Carefully place over the lighted spirit stove and heat gently.

Toss the cheeses in the cornflour then gradually add them to the apple juice, stirring continuously.

When all the cheese has been added, stir in the honey and add pepper to taste. Cook, stirring until thick and creamy.

Stir the chopped watercress into the fondue and serve with the dippers and salad.

AVOCADO & PECAN FONDUE

LOOK FOR AVOCADOS THAT ARE RIPE, BUT NOT REALLY SOFT, OTHERWISE THE COLOUR OF THE FONDUE WILL NOT BE GOOD.

Serves **4 to 6**
Preparation time **12 to 15 minutes**
Cooking time **15 minutes**

6 spring onions, chopped
250 ml/8 fl oz dry white wine
2 large ripe avocados
2 Tbsp lemon juice
300 g/10 oz Gruyère cheese, grated
100 g/4 oz blue cheese, such as Gorgonzola, crumbled
1 Tbsp cornflour

50 g/2 oz chopped pecan nuts
3 Tbsp single cream
Freshly grated nutmeg

TO SERVE

Breadsticks, pretzels, cooked king-size prawns, melon and fresh pear wedges for dipping. Artichoke & Bean Salad with Vinaigrette (*see page 110*), Tossed Green Salad (*see page 114*), and freshly cooked potato skins

Gently sauté the spring onions in the wine for 3 minutes.

Peel and halve the avocados and discard the stones. Mash the flesh with the lemon juice and set aside.

Toss the cheeses in the cornflour, then slowly stir into the fondue pot. Cook, stirring, until the cheese has melted.

Stir the mashed avocado into the fondue, then stir in the pecan nuts and cream. Add nutmeg to taste. Cook, stirring until thickened. Serve with the dippers, salads and potato skins.

ASIAN VEGETABLE FONDUE

IT IS POSSIBLE TO BUY READY-PREPARED *DIM SUM* SNACKS, WHICH WOULD BE IDEAL TO SERVE AS DIPPERS FOR THIS FONDUE. ADDING A LITTLE SESAME OIL TO THE COOKING OIL WILL HELP TO GIVE AN ASIAN FLAVOUR.

Prepare the vegetables, cutting them into thin strips or chunks where necessary. If you prefer a softer vegetable, dip in boiling water for 3 to 5 minutes after cooking, drain and arrange in small bowls. Cut the tofu into cubes and arrange in small bowls.

Using a whisk, blend the egg yolk with the water, flour and a teaspoon of the sesame oil until smooth. Whisk the egg white until stiff, then stir into the batter, cover and leave for 30 minutes.

Heat the oil and the remaining sesame oil in a Mongolian hot pot or fondue pot and carefully place over the lighted spirit stove.

Spear the vegetables and tofu cubes on to the fondue forks and dip into the prepared batter, then into the hot oil. Cook for 2 to 3 minutes or until golden. Spear the dim sum on to the fondue forks and without first dipping into the batter, cook in the hot oil.

Garnish with the chopped spring onions and serve with the dipping sauces, salad and glutinous rice.

Serves **6**
Preparation time **15 minutes**
  plus 30 minutes standing time
  for the batter
Cooking time **2 to 3 minutes**
  per vegetable

100 g/4 oz baby sweetcorn
100 g/4 oz small asparagus spears
175 g/6 oz water chestnuts
1 red pepper, deseeded
1 yellow pepper, deseeded
100 g/4 oz bamboo shoots
175 g/6 oz firm tofu
1 medium egg, separated
250 ml/¼ pt ice-cold water
100 g/4 oz plain flour
3 tsp sesame oil
600 ml/1 pt oil, for frying
1 packet prepared *dim sum*, optional

TO GARNISH
Chopped spring onions

TO SERVE
Soy sauce, hoisin sauce, Sweet & Sour Sauce *(see page 97)*, **Mixed Chinese Green Salad** *(see page 108)* **and freshly cooked glutinous (short-grain) rice**

SPINACH FONDUE

FRESH SPINACH IS READILY AVAILABLE IN MOST FRESH PRODUCE MARKETS. HOWEVER, USING THE FROZEN VARIETY SAVES TIME AS IT IS ALREADY WASHED AND CHOPPED. IF USING FROZEN SPINACH WITH THIS FONDUE, FIRST THAW IT AND SQUEEZE OUT ANY EXCESS MOISTURE.

Melt the butter in the fondue pot and gently sauté the onion and garlic for 5 minutes, or until softened. Add the cider and heat through, then carefully place over the lighted spirit stove.

Toss the cheeses in the cornflour then stir into the fondue pot. Squeeze any excess moisture from the spinach and chop finely. Add to the fondue pot and cook until the mixture is smooth and creamy.

Stir in the lemon zest, juice, honey and black pepper to taste, and continue to heat for 5 minutes before serving with the dippers and salads.

Serves **5 to 6**
Preparation time **15 minutes**
Cooking time **12 to 15 minutes**

50 g/2 oz butter
1 medium onion, finely chopped
2 to 3 garlic cloves, crushed
300 ml/$\frac{1}{2}$ pt dry cider
225 g/8 oz Emmental cheese, grated
100 g/4 oz Gorgonzola cheese, crumbled
2 Tbsp cornflour
225 g/8 oz thawed frozen spinach
1 Tbsp grated lemon zest
2 to 3 Tbsp lemon juice
1 to 2 tsp clear honey or to taste
Freshly ground black pepper

TO SERVE

Breadsticks, celery and apple wedges, cubes
   of salami and chipolata sausages, for dipping.
   Artichoke & Bean Salad with Vinaigrette *(see page 113)* and Zesty Orange Coleslaw *(see page 114)*

ONION & CARAWAY FONDUE

LOOK FOR THE DIFFERENT VARIETIES OF ONIONS THAT ARE NOW AVAILABLE. I LIKE WHITE ONIONS AS THEY ARE SWEETER THAN YELLOW ONIONS.

Serves **4**
Preparation time **10 minutes**
Cooking time **20 minutes**

50 g/2 oz butter
450 g/1 lb onions, chopped
2 to 3 garlic cloves, peeled and crushed
1 to 2 tsp caraway seeds
150 ml/¼ pt dry white wine
300 g/10 oz Gruyère cheese, grated
100 g/4 oz feta cheese, crumbled
2 Tbsp cornflour

1 tsp wholegrain mustard
Freshly ground black pepper
¼ tsp grated nutmeg

TO SERVE
Frankfurter sausages, pepperoni sticks, cubes of pumpernickel bread and pretzels for dipping. Sauerkraut Salad *(see page 107)*, Tossed Green Salad *(see page 114)* and Creamy Potato & Apple Salad *(see page 117)*

Melt the butter in the fondue pot, then gently sauté the onions and garlic for 10 to 15 minutes or until softened. Stir in the caraway seeds and cook for 2 minutes. Add the wine and heat through, then place over the lighted spirit stove.

Toss the cheeses in the cornflour then gradually stir into the fondue pot and continue stirring until all the cheese has melted.

Stir in the mustard, add pepper to taste and add the nutmeg. Heat through gently until the mixture is thick and creamy. Serve with the dippers and salads.

ASPARAGUS FONDUE

THIS FONDUE IS VERY QUICK TO MAKE, AND IS IDEAL TO SERVE WHEN FRIENDS VISIT UNEXPECTEDLY.

Serves **4**
Preparation time **10 minutes**
Cooking time **15 minutes**

2 to 3 garlic cloves, crushed
6 to 8 fresh asparagus spears, chopped
300 ml/½ pt apple juice
2 Tbsp medium-dry sherry
350 g/12 oz Emmental cheese, grated
2 Tbsp cornflour
Tabasco Sauce, to taste
Freshly ground black pepper

TO SERVE
Fresh blanched asparagus spears, cucumber and carrot sticks, and artichoke hearts for dipping. Freshly cooked new potatoes and Tossed Green Salad *(see page 114)*

In a pan, gently sauté the garlic and asparagus in the apple juice for 5 minutes, or until softened. Add the sherry. Stir gently until well blended and hot, then pour into the fondue pot and carefully place over the lighted spirit stove.

Toss the cheese in the cornflour then stir into the pot and cook, stirring until the cheese has melted. Season to taste with the Tabasco Sauce and black pepper, and cook until thick and creamy. Serve with the dippers, potatoes and salad.

MIXED VEGETABLE FONDUE

WHEN CHOOSING THE VEGETABLES FOR THIS FONDUE, SELECT A GOOD VARIETY OF COLOURS, SHAPES AND TEXTURES, TO MAKE AN ATTRACTIVE AND APPEALING MEAL.

Using a whisk, blend the egg yolk with the water, apple juice, flour and olive oil until smooth. Whisk the egg white until stiff. Stir into the batter, cover and stand for at least 30 minutes.

Prepare the vegetables, dividing the cauliflower and broccoli into small florets. Blanch in boiling water for 2 minutes, drain and refresh in cold water, then drain thoroughly and pat dry with kitchen paper. Wash and pat the pepper strips dry. Rinse and dry the courgette strips. Dip the carrot strips in boiling water for 2 minutes, then drain and pat dry. Wash the artichoke hearts and pat dry with kitchen paper. Wipe the mushrooms well.

Heat the oil in the fondue pot, then carefully place over the lighted spirit stove.

Dip the prepared vegetables into the batter, and spear on to fondue forks. Cook in the hot oil for 2 to 3 minutes or until golden. Serve with the dipping sauces, salad and potatoes.

Serves **6**
Preparation time **15 minutes plus 30 minutes standing time for batter**
Cooking time **2 to 3 minutes per vegetable**

1 small egg, separated
175 ml/6 fl oz ice-cold water
50 ml/2 fl oz apple juice
100 g/4 oz plain flour
1 tsp olive oil
675 g/1½ lb assorted vegetables, such as cauliflower and broccoli florets, strips of assorted peppers, courgette and carrot sticks, artichoke hearts and mushrooms
600 ml/1 pt oil, for frying

TO SERVE
Blue Cheese Dressing *(see page 96)*, **Salsa** *(see page 99)*, **Madeira Sauce** *(see page 103)*, **Spiced Rice Salad** *(see page 109)* **and freshly cooked new potatoes**

GUACAMOLE FONDUE

AVOCADOS HAVE A WONDERFUL CREAMY TEXTURE AND A NUTTY FLAVOUR. TO PREVENT THE FONDUE FROM DISCOLOURING, PREPARE IT AT THE VERY LAST MOMENT AND MIX WITH LEMON OR LIME JUICE.

Cut the garlic and rub it on the insides of the fondue pot, then pour in the white wine. Carefully place over the lighted spirit stove and heat gently. Toss the cheeses in the cornflour, then gradually stir them into the wine. Heat gently, stirring throughout until the cheese has melted, then stir in the tomato purée.

Peel and stone the avocado and mash well, pour over the lemon or lime juice and mix lightly. Stir into the cheese mixture with the soured cream. Add black pepper to taste. Heat gently, stirring until the mixture is thick and creamy. Serve with the dippers, dipping sauces and salad.

Serves **4 to 6**
Preparation time **10 to 15 minutes**
Cooking time **10 minutes**

1 garlic clove
150 ml/¼ pt dry white wine
350 g/12 oz Gruyère cheese, grated
100 g/4 oz feta cheese, crumbled
2 Tbsp cornflour
2 Tbsp tomato purée
1 large avocado
3 Tbsp lemon or lime juice
3 Tbsp soured cream
Freshly ground black pepper

TO SERVE
Avocado wedges tossed in lemon juice, pickled jalapeño chillies, red pepper strips and strips of warm pitta bread for dipping. Salsa *(see page 99)*, Soured Cream Sauce *(see page 103)* and Tossed Green Salad *(see page 114)*

SAUCES & DIPS

BLUE CHEESE DRESSING

I HAVE USED ROQUEFORT CHEESE IN THIS RECIPE, BUT YOU CAN USE ANY BLUE CHEESE. LOOK FOR A CREAMY CHEESE THAT WILL BREAK DOWN EASILY AND COMBINE WELL WITH THE OTHER INGREDIENTS.

Makes **350 ml/ 12 fl oz**

Preparation time **5 minutes**

Chilling time **30 minutes**

250 ml/8 fl oz soured cream
3 Tbsp low-fat natural yoghurt
75 g/3 oz Roquefort cheese
2 Tbsp lemon juice
2 tsp brandy, optional
2 Tbsp snipped fresh chives
Salt and freshly ground black pepper

Place the soured cream in a bowl and stir in the yoghurt. Crumble the cheese, then stir into the soured cream mixture.

Add the remaining ingredients, then turn into a serving bowl, cover and chill in the fridge for 30 minutes before serving.

GREEN MAYONNAISE

ALTHOUGH SOME COMMERCIALLY MADE MAYONNAISE IS GOOD, NOTHING COMPARES WITH THE GENUINE ARTICLE. IF YOU DO NOT HAVE A FOOD PROCESSOR, YOU CAN BEAT THE INGREDIENTS BY HAND.

Makes **250 ml/ 8 fl oz**

Preparation time **5 to 6 minutes**

1 egg yolk
$\frac{1}{2}$ tsp salt
$\frac{1}{2}$ tsp dry mustard powder
Freshly ground black pepper
$\frac{1}{2}$ tsp caster sugar
150 ml/$\frac{1}{4}$ pt olive oil
1 to 2 Tbsp lemon juice
2 shallots, peeled and finely chopped
4 Tbsp fresh watercress, chopped
1 Tbsp fresh parsley, chopped
2 Tbsp toasted pine nuts, chopped

Place the egg yolk with the seasonings and sugar in the bowl of the food processor and switch on. Keeping the speed low, gradually add the oil, a little at a time.

Once all the oil has been added, slowly add the lemon juice.

Stir in the chopped shallots, watercress, parsley and pine nuts. Turn into a serving bowl, cover and store in the fridge until required. Stir before using.

SWEET & SOUR SAUCE

THE TANG IN THIS SAUCE IS ESPECIALLY GOOD WITH RICH FOODS SUCH AS PORK AND OILY FISH. IT IS ALSO DELICIOUS WITH CHICKEN AND TURKEY DISHES.

Heat the oil in a pan and gently sauté the pepper and spring onions for 3 minutes.

Add the chicken stock, soy sauce, vinegar, ginger and honey, then simmer for 3 minutes. Bring to the boil.

Blend the cornflour with the pineapple juice, stir into the sauce and cook, stirring until the sauce thickens. Serve.

Makes **475 ml/16 fl oz**
Preparation time **5 to 7 minutes**
Cooking time **8 to 10 minutes**

1 Tbsp oil

1 red pepper, deseeded and chopped

6 spring onions, trimmed and chopped

150 ml/¼ pt chicken stock

1 Tbsp dark soy sauce

1 Tbsp red wine vinegar

2 Tbsp stem ginger, chopped

1 to 2 tsp clear honey

2 Tbsp cornflour

85 ml/3 fl oz pineapple juice

QUICK SATAY SAUCE

A SPEEDY ALTERNATIVE TO THE STANDARD SATAY SAUCE, THIS VERSION IS MADE IN A MATTER OF MINUTES.

Blend all the ingredients, except the coconut milk, until smooth. Slowly stir in the coconut milk, then pour into a pan and heat gently.

Cook gently for about 2 to 4 minutes or until heated. Serve warm or cold, according to preference.

Makes **300 ml/½ pt**
Preparation time **3 to 4 minutes**
Cooking time **2 to 4 minutes**

6 Tbsp smooth or crunchy peanut butter
½ tsp hot chilli powder
½ tsp ground ginger
2 Tbsp lemon juice
1 Tbsp dark soy sauce
150 ml/¼ pt coconut milk

SATAY SAUCE

THIS IS RAPIDLY BECOMING A VERY POPULAR
CHOICE AND CAN BE USED AS A SAUCE OR
DIP, AS WELL AS A MARINADE FOR FISH, POULTRY,
MEATS OR VEGETABLE CRUDITÉS.

Makes **475 ml/**	**2 Tbsp oil**
16 fl oz	**2 medium onions, chopped or grated**
Preparation time	**2 to 3 garlic cloves, crushed**
8 minutes	**½ to 1 tsp hot chilli powder**
Cooking time	**75 g/3 oz roasted peanuts**
10 to 11 minutes	**150 ml/¼ pt warm water**
	1 Tbsp granulated brown sugar
	1 Tbsp lemon juice
	1 Tbsp dark soy sauce

Heat the oil, then add one of the onions and fry for 5 minutes
or until soft.

Place the remaining onion with the garlic, chilli powder
and peanuts in a food processor and blend to form a paste.

Gradually stir the paste into the cooked onion and cook for
2 to 3 minutes. Slowly stir in the water, then add the sugar,
lemon juice and soy sauce. Bring to the boil and boil gently for
2 minutes or until a chunky sauce is formed. Serve.

SALSA

ADD FRESH FRUITS, VEGETABLES AND SPICES
TO THE BASIC RECIPE BELOW FOR DIFFERENT
SALSA COMBINATIONS.

Makes **200 ml/7 fl oz**	**225 g/8 oz ripe tomatoes, peeled and**
Preparation time	**deseeded**
6 to 8 minutes	**1 to 2 jalapeño chillies, deseeded and**
Chilling time	**chopped**
30 minutes	**4 spring onions, chopped**
	1 to 2 tsp warmed clear honey
	2 Tbsp chopped fresh coriander
	Salt and freshly ground black pepper
	5 cm/2 inch piece of cucumber, skinned and
	deseeded

Finely chop the tomatoes and place in a bowl with the chillies,
spring onions, honey and coriander. Season to taste.

Finely chop the cucumber and stir into the salsa. Spoon into a
serving bowl, cover and chill for 30 minutes.

VARIATIONS
Add a small, ripe, peeled and chopped mango to the basic salsa
and stir in a tablespoon of toasted sesame seeds.

Toss a ripe, peeled and diced avocado in 2 tablespoons of lemon
juice and stir into the basic salsa recipe.

Substitute 225 g/8 oz of peeled, deseeded and chopped green
tomatillos for the ripe tomatoes; then cook gently in 2 tablespoons
of white wine. Add to the basic salsa with 2 tablespoons of raisins.

TARTARE SAUCE

TARTARE SAUCE COMBINES WELL WITH ALL KINDS OF FISH, VEGETABLES AND SOME POULTRY DISHES. IT CAN BE MADE AHEAD OF TIME, THEN STORED FOR UP TO TWO DAYS IF COVERED AND KEPT IN THE FRIDGE.

Makes **200 ml/7 fl oz**
Preparation time
 6 to 8 minutes

1 egg yolk
$\frac{1}{2}$ tsp mustard powder
$\frac{1}{2}$ tsp salt
Freshly ground black pepper
$\frac{1}{2}$ tsp caster sugar
150 ml/$\frac{1}{4}$ pt olive oil
1 Tbsp white wine vinegar
2 tsp chopped fresh tarragon
2 tsp chopped fresh parsley
1 Tbsp chopped capers
1 Tbsp chopped gherkins
1 to 2 Tbsp lemon juice

Place the egg yolk in a bowl with the mustard, salt, black pepper to taste and sugar. Mix well, then very slowly add the oil, drop by drop, all the time whisking well. Continue to whisk until a thick and smooth sauce is formed.

When all the oil has been added, stir in the white wine vinegar, chopped herbs, capers, gherkins and lemon juice. Stir until blended, then spoon into a bowl, cover and leave for about 1 hour to allow the flavours to develop. Serve.

GREEN TOMATILLO SAUCE

TOMATILLOS ARE A VARIETY OF GREEN TOMATO WITH INFLATED PAPERY SKINS. THEY HAVE A BITTER FLAVOUR WITH OVERTONES OF LEMON. THE BITTERNESS IS LOST WHEN THE FRUIT IS COOKED. TINNED TOMATILLOS CAN BE BOUGHT IN SPECIALIST FOOD SHOPS. YOU CAN SUBSTITUTE GREEN TOMATOES IF TOMATILLOS ARE NOT AVAILABLE, BUT ADD A LITTLE LEMON JUICE TO RE-CREATE THE LEMONY FLAVOUR.

Makes **300 ml/$\frac{1}{2}$ pt**
Preparation time
 8 minutes
Cooking time
 15 minutes

1 Tbsp oil
1 to 2 garlic cloves, crushed
1 to 2 red serrano chillies, chopped
 and deseeded
300 g/10 oz tomatillos, chopped
150 ml/$\frac{1}{4}$ pt vegetable stock
1 to 2 tsp clear honey
Salt and freshly ground black pepper
2 Tbsp chopped fresh coriander
2 Tbsp lime juice
1 to 1$\frac{1}{2}$ Tbsp arrowroot

Heat the oil in a pan and gently sauté the garlic, chillies and tomatillos for 5 minutes. Add the stock and honey, season to taste, then simmer for 10 minutes or until the tomatillos are soft and pulpy.

Rub through a fine-meshed sieve and return to the cleaned pan. Add the coriander, blend the lime juice and arrowroot together and stir into the pan. Cook, stirring, until the sauce thickens and clears. Adjust the seasoning and serve warm or cold.

TOMATO DEVILLED SAUCE

THERE ARE MANY READY-PREPARED MUSTARDS NOW COMMERCIALLY AVAILABLE. HOWEVER, FOR DEPTH OF FLAVOUR AND GREATER CONTROL, I PREFER TO USE MUSTARD POWDER AS IT ONLY BECOMES FIERCE WHEN MIXED TO A PASTE WITH WATER.

Melt the butter in a pan and gently sauté the onion, chilli, and garlic for 3 minutes. Add the chopped pepper with the mustard powder and flour, and cook for a further 2 minutes.

Add the tomatoes, then blend the tomato purée with the stock or water, and add to the pan with the Worcestershire sauce. Bring to the boil, then cover and simmer for 10 minutes, stirring occasionally.

Add the seasoning to taste, stir well and serve the sauce hot.

Makes **350 g/12 fl oz**
Preparation time **6 to 8 minutes**
Cooking time **15 minutes**

1 Tbsp butter
1 small onion, chopped
1 red serrano chilli, deseeded and
  chopped
1 to 2 garlic cloves, crushed
1 small red pepper, deseeded and
  chopped
1 to 3 tsp mustard powder
1 Tbsp plain flour
225 g/8 oz tomatoes, peeled and chopped
1 Tbsp tomato purée
4 Tbsp stock or water
1 to 2 tsp Worcestershire sauce
Salt and freshly ground black pepper

ORANGE CUMBERLAND
DIPPING SAUCE

USE A ZESTER IF YOU HAVE ONE TO REMOVE THE ZEST FROM THE ORANGE AND LEMON.
IF NOT, REMOVE AS FINE A LAYER OF PEEL AS POSSIBLE AND CUT INTO VERY THIN STRIPS.
BLANCH THESE FOR A LITTLE LONGER.

Remove the zest from the orange and lemon, slice finely and blanch in boiling water for 1 to 3 minutes (depending on thickness). Remove and refresh in cold water. Drain and reserve.

Squeeze the juice from the fruits and strain into a pan. Add the marmalade, red wine, sugar and seasoning to taste.

Bring to the boil. Blend the arrowroot with 1 tablespoon of water, then stir into the pan. Cook, stirring until the sauce thickens and clears. Stir in the reserved blanched fruit zest and serve.

Makes **250 ml/8 fl oz**
Preparation time **5 minutes**
Cooking time **5 minutes**

1 orange
1 lemon
6 Tbsp orange marmalade
4 Tbsp red wine
2 Tbsp granulated light brown sugar
Salt and freshly ground black pepper
1 tsp arrowroot

MADEIRA SAUCE

WHENEVER I OPEN A BOTTLE OF MADEIRA OR PORT, I ALWAYS TRY TO FIND A WAY OF USING IT UP FAIRLY QUICKLY, AS THESE DRINKS DO NOT LAST LONG ONCE OPENED. A GOOD WAY TO DO THIS IS BY MAKING THE FOLLOWING SAUCE, WHICH HAS NOW BECOME A FAVOURITE OF MINE.

Makes **300 ml/½ pt**
Preparation time
5 minutes
Cooking time
10 minutes

1 Tbsp butter
50 g/2 oz mushrooms, finely chopped
100 g/4 oz tomatoes, peeled, deseeded and chopped
1 Tbsp plain flour
150 ml/¼ pt Madeira
2 Tbsp orange juice
1 Tbsp clear honey
Salt and freshly ground black pepper

Melt the butter in a pan and gently sauté the mushrooms for 5 minutes. Add the tomatoes and continue to cook for 2 minutes.

Sprinkle in the flour and cook for 2 minutes, then take the pan off the heat and gradually stir in the Madeira before adding the orange juice.

Return to the heat and cook, stirring, until the sauce thickens. Stir in the honey with seasoning to taste.

Simmer for 2 minutes, and serve.

SOURED CREAM SAUCE

THIS SAUCE IS IDEAL SERVED WITH STEAKS AND LAMB DISHES. FOR A HEALTHIER VERSION SUBSTITUTE LOW-FAT NATURAL OR GREEK YOGHURT FOR HALF THE SOURED CREAM. SHERRY, WHITE WINE, OR RASPBERRY VINEGAR CAN BE USED IN PLACE OF THE TARRAGON VINEGAR.

Makes **200 ml/7 fl oz**
Preparation time
5 minutes plus
30 minutes
marinating time

150 ml/¼ pt soured cream
1 small onion, finely chopped
1 Tbsp chopped capers
¼ tsp salt
½ tsp freshly ground black pepper
1 Tbsp chopped fresh parsley
2 Tbsp tarragon vinegar

Place the soured cream into a bowl, then stir in the onion, capers, salt and pepper. Add the parsley, then slowly stir in the vinegar until well blended.

Turn into a serving bowl, cover and leave in the fridge for at least 30 minutes to allow the flavours to develop.

INDIAN-STYLE RAITA

THIS SAUCE IS SMOOTH, CREAMY AND VERY COOL ON THE PALATE. IT IS IDEAL SERVED WITH HOT, SPICY DISHES OR WHEN THE WEATHER IS REALLY HOT.

Makes **350 ml/ 12 fl oz**
Preparation time **5 minutes**
Chilling time **30 minutes**

300 ml/$\frac{1}{2}$ pt low-fat natural yoghurt
7.5 cm/3 inch piece of cucumber
2 Tbsp chopped fresh coriander
1 Tbsp chopped fresh parsley
1 Tbsp grated lime zest
Salt and freshly ground black pepper

Place the yoghurt into a small bowl. Thinly peel the cucumber and discard the seeds. Finely dice the flesh.

Add the cucumber to the yoghurt and stir in the chopped herbs, lime zest, and seasoning to taste. Lightly mix together.

Spoon into a serving bowl and cover lightly. Chill in the fridge for 30 minutes before serving.

CREAMY HERB MAYONNAISE

VARY THE HERBS ACCORDING TO THE FOOD BEING SERVED. DIFFERENT HERBS MARRY WELL WITH DIFFERENT FOODS (SEE BELOW).

Makes **250 ml/8 fl oz**
Preparation time **8 to 9 minutes**

2 egg yolks
$\frac{1}{2}$ tsp wholegrain mustard
$\frac{1}{2}$ tsp salt
$\frac{1}{2}$ tsp freshly ground black pepper
$\frac{1}{2}$ tsp caster sugar
150 ml/$\frac{1}{4}$ pt olive oil
2 Tbsp lemon juice
2 Tbsp chopped fresh herbs (see below)
1 egg white

Beat the egg yolks with the mustard, seasonings and sugar then add the oil drop by drop, beating vigorously until the mayonnaise is smooth and creamy.

Stir in the lemon juice with the chopped fresh herbs, cover and leave in the fridge until required. Just before serving, whisk the egg white until stiff, stir into the mayonnaise and serve.

Try dill, tarragon, parsley and chives with fish. With poultry use a few of the following: chervil, parsley, coriander, tarragon, basil and sage. With steak use sage, thyme, oregano and rosemary. With pork, use a few of the following: sage, thyme, oregano, parsley and coriander. Lamb goes well with rosemary, basil, oregano, marjoram and coriander.

SALADS

AVOCADO & MANGO SALAD

MANY FONDUES ARE QUITE RICH AND A FRESH, CRISP SALAD MAKES AN IDEAL ACCOMPANIMENT. THIS SALAD, WITH
ITS BITTER SALAD LEAVES, IS WONDERFUL SERVED WITH RICH CHEESE FONDUES.

Serves **4**
Preparation time **8 to 10 minutes**

1 large, ripe avocado

2 Tbsp lime juice

1 large, ripe mango

100 g/4 oz bitter salad leaves such as radicchio,
   rocket, baby spinach leaves, frisée

6 spring onions, trimmed and chopped

100 g/4 oz cherry tomatoes, quartered

25 g/1 oz toasted pine nuts

DRESSING

3 Tbsp olive oil

1 Tbsp walnut oil

2 Tbsp orange juice

Salt and freshly ground black pepper

1 tsp wholegrain mustard

1 to 2 tsp clear honey

Peel and stone the avocado, then slice and toss in the lime juice. Peel the mango and slice thinly.

Rinse the salad leaves, shake off the excess water and place in a salad bowl. Arrange the sliced avocado, mango, spring onions and tomatoes on top, then toss lightly together. Sprinkle over the toasted pine nuts. Place all the ingredients for the dressing together in a screwtop jar and shake vigorously. Pour over the salad and serve.

SAUERKRAUT SALAD

IF YOU FIND SAUERKRAUT IS USUALLY TOO SHARP FOR YOUR PALATE, ADD A LITTLE EXTRA HONEY TO THE DRESSING—YOU WILL BE PLEASANTLY SURPRISED AT THE DIFFERENCE THIS WILL MAKE.

Serves **6**
Preparation time
   5 to 8 minutes

450 g/1 lb prepared
   sauerkraut, fresh or tinned

1 medium onion, finely
   chopped

4 large gherkins

2 red dessert apples

2 Tbsp lemon juice

1 Tbsp chopped fresh parsley

1 Tbsp chopped fresh basil

DRESSING

5 Tbsp olive oil

2 Tbsp lemon juice

2 to 3 tsp clear honey

Salt and freshly ground
   black pepper

1 tsp caraway seeds

Drain the sauerkraut, rinse thoroughly and dry well on kitchen paper. Place in a bowl with the chopped onion.

Finely chop the gherkins and add to the bowl. Wash, core and chop the apples and toss in the lemon juice, then add to the bowl with the chopped herbs.

Place all the ingredients for the dressing in a screwtop jar and shake vigorously, then pour over the salad and serve.

MIXED CHINESE GREEN SALAD

AS WITH MOST SALADS, THIS IS BEST MADE JUST BEFORE IT IS REQUIRED. TOSS IN THE DRESSING AND THEN SERVE.

Place the bok choy in a large bowl with the spring onions. Thinly peel the cucumber and cut into half-moon shapes, and add to the bok choy with the celery, pepper and bean sprouts.

Make the dressing by placing all the ingredients in a screwtop jar. Shake vigorously until well blended.

Just before serving, toss the salad in the prepared dressing, place in a serving bowl and sprinkle with the chopped coriander and peanuts.

Serves **6**
Preparation time **5 to 6 minutes**

200 g/7 oz bok choy, rinsed and finely shredded
8 spring onions, trimmed and chopped
½ small cucumber
4 celery sticks, trimmed and chopped
1 green pepper, deseeded and sliced
100 g/4 oz bean sprouts
2 Tbsp chopped fresh coriander
2 Tbsp unsalted roasted peanuts, roughly chopped

DRESSING
4 Tbsp oil
1 tsp sesame oil
1 Tbsp dark soy sauce
2 Tbsp orange juice
Salt and freshly ground black pepper

CHILLED RATATOUILLE

IF YOU ARE PLANNING AN INFORMAL FONDUE, WITH FRIENDS SITTING IN THE LIVING ROOM OR OUTSIDE, IT WILL BE EASIER TO EAT SALADS THAT ARE CUT INTO BITE-SIZED PIECES.

Serves **4 to 6**
Preparation time
  12 to 15 minutes plus
  30 minutes chilling time
Cooking time **20 minutes**

4 Tbsp olive oil
1 medium onion, peeled and sliced
2 to 3 garlic cloves, crushed
1 medium aubergine, cubed
1 red pepper, deseeded and sliced
1 yellow pepper, deseeded
  and sliced
1 courgette, sliced
225 g/8 oz tomatoes, chopped
100 g/4 oz mushrooms, sliced
3 Tbsp white wine
Salt and freshly ground black pepper
2 Tbsp chopped fresh basil

Heat the oil in a large pan and sauté the onion, garlic and aubergine for 5 minutes. Add the peppers, courgette, tomatoes, mushrooms and white wine, cover with a lid and cook gently for 10 minutes, stirring occasionally.

Season to taste, and continue to cook gently for 5 minutes or until the vegetables are tender but still retaining their shape.

Cool, chill for at least 30 minutes and serve sprinkled with the chopped basil.

SPICED RICE SALAD

CHOOSE YOUR FAVOURITE KIND OF RICE FOR THIS SALAD. A MIXTURE OF WHITE RICE AND WILD, OR THAI RICE GO PARTICULARLY WELL.

Serves **6**
Preparation time **10 minutes**
Cooking time **15 to 18 minutes**

175 g/6 oz rice (see above)
1 tsp ground cumin
$\frac{1}{2}$ tsp ground coriander
2 large carrots, peeled and grated
8 spring onions, trimmed and
  chopped
1 red pepper, deseeded and
  chopped
100 g/4 oz raisins
2 Tbsp chopped fresh coriander

DRESSING
4 Tbsp olive oil
2 Tbsp orange juice
$\frac{1}{2}$ tsp ground coriander
$\frac{1}{2}$ to 1 tsp crushed chillies
Salt and freshly ground
  black pepper

Cook the rice in lightly salted boiling water for 15 to 18 minutes, or until cooked. Drain and place in a bowl. Add the ground cumin and coriander.

Stir in the carrots, spring onions, pepper, raisins and chopped coriander. Lightly toss together.

Place all the ingredients for the dressing in a screwtop jar and shake vigorously, then pour over the salad and serve.

ARTICHOKE & BEAN SALAD WITH
VINAIGRETTE

USE EITHER ARTICHOKE HEARTS OR BOTTOMS FOR THIS BEAN SALAD. WHICHEVER YOU USE, THE RESULT
WILL BE DELICIOUS.

Trim the beans, cut into short lengths and cook in lightly salted boiling water for 5 to 7 minutes or until tender but still retaining some crispness. Drain and refresh in cold water. Drain and place in a bowl.

Drain all the canned beans and rinse, then add to the French beans with the artichoke hearts or bottoms, olives and spring onions.

Blend the dressing ingredients, pour over the salad, stir lightly and serve.

Serves **6**
Preparation time **8 to 10 minutes**
Cooking time **5 to 7 minutes**

300 g/10 oz French beans
400 g/14 oz tinned cannellini beans
200 g/7 oz tinned red kidney beans
400 g/14 oz tinned artichoke hearts
  or bottoms
75 g/3 oz green and black olives,
  stoned
6 spring onions, trimmed and
  chopped

DRESSING
6 Tbsp olive oil
2 Tbsp white wine vinegar
1 tsp caster sugar
Salt and freshly ground
  black pepper
1 Tbsp chopped fresh parsley
1 Tbsp chopped fresh coriander

TO GARNISH
Fresh coriander sprigs

MEDITERRANEAN SALAD

IF YOU ARE LUCKY ENOUGH TO LIVE NEAR A GOOD DELI, LOOK FOR LARGE, PLUMP, MARINATED OLIVES FOR THIS SALAD. THERE ARE MANY VARIETIES AVAILABLE—ALL DELICIOUS—THE ONLY PROBLEM IS THAT YOU WILL NEED TO BUY DOUBLE THE AMOUNT CALLED FOR, TO ALLOW FOR INEVITABLE SNACKING!

Place the artichoke hearts in a bowl. Rinse the tomatoes and halve, then add to the bowl.

Wipe the mushrooms and cut in half, or slice if large, and add to the bowl with the olives.

Place all the ingredients for the dressing in a bowl, and whisk until smooth.

Line the salad bowl with the rinsed salad leaves, then place the salad ingredients in the centre. Sprinkle with the rock salt and chopped parsley and serve with the salad dressing.

Serves **4 to 6**
Preparation time **5 to 8 minutes**

450 g/1 lb tinned artichoke hearts, drained and sliced
100 g/4 oz cherry tomatoes
100 g/4 oz baby button mushrooms
75 g/3 oz black olives, stoned
175 g/6 oz assorted salad leaves
Rock salt
2 Tbsp chopped fresh flat-leaf parsley

DRESSING
150 ml/$\frac{1}{4}$ pt soured cream
1 to 2 tsp Dijon mustard
2 Tbsp olive oil
1 onion, finely chopped
2 Tbsp capers
1 tsp caster sugar

ZESTY ORANGE COLESLAW

IF YOU HAVE A FOOD PROCESSOR WITH A SHREDDER OR GRATING ATTACHMENT, USE IT TO SHRED THE CABBAGE. IT SPEEDS UP THE MAKING OF THE COLESLAW CONSIDERABLY.

Serves **6 to 8**
Preparation time **12 minutes**

450 g/1 lb fresh white inner cabbage leaves, finely shredded
2 large carrots
2 large oranges
1 orange pepper, deseeded and chopped
100 g/4 oz yellow cherry tomatoes
75 g/3 oz sultanas
2 Tbsp chopped fresh flat-leaf parsley

DRESSING

6 Tbsp olive oil
2 Tbsp orange juice
1 Tbsp grated orange zest
1 tsp prepared mustard
Salt and freshly ground black pepper

Place the cabbage in a bowl.

Peel and grate the carrot, peel and divide the oranges into segments, then cut the segments into small pieces. Add the carrot, orange pepper, tomatoes and sultanas to the cabbage. Toss lightly.

Place all the ingredients for the dressing in a screwtop jar and shake vigorously. Pour over the cabbage mixture, toss lightly then turn into a salad bowl. Sprinkle with the chopped flat-leaf parsley, and serve.

TOSSED GREEN SALAD

CHEESE-BASED FONDUES ARE FILLING, SO A GREEN SALAD AND SOME CRUSTY BREAD ARE OFTEN THE ONLY ACCOMPANIMENTS NEEDED.

Serves **4**
Preparation time **10 to 12 minutes**

1 garlic clove, halved
1 Romaine lettuce
½ small cucumber
3 celery sticks, trimmed and chopped
1 green pepper, deseeded
2 chicory heads
6 spring onions, trimmed
1 large, ripe avocado
2 Tbsp lemon juice
2 Tbsp roughly chopped parsley

DRESSING

5 Tbsp olive oil
2 Tbsp white wine vinegar
1 tsp Dijon mustard
Salt and freshly ground black pepper
1 to 2 tsp caster sugar

Rub the garlic inside the salad bowl. Rinse the lettuce leaves, pat dry, tear into small pieces and place in the bowl.

Peel and dice the cucumber. Add to the lettuce with the celery.

Slice the pepper into half-moon shapes, and add to the bowl. Pull the chicory heads apart, rinse then arrange in the bowl.

Chop the spring onions and scatter over the lettuce. Peel the avocado and discard the stone, dice, toss in the lemon juice then arrange in the salad bowl with the parsley.

Place all the dressing ingredients in a screwtop jar. Shake vigorously until well blended. Pour over the salad, toss and serve.

ARTICHOKE HEART SALAD

A VARIATION ON THE EVER-POPULAR WALDORF SALAD, THIS SALAD IS SURE TO BECOME A FAVOURITE WITH YOUR FRIENDS AND FAMILY, AS IT HAS WITH MINE. IF YOU PREFER, THE ARTICHOKE HEARTS CAN BE REPLACED WITH TINNED WHITE ASPARAGUS OR PALM HEARTS.

Drain the artichoke hearts and chop into bite-sized pieces. Rinse the lettuce, drain well and arrange in a salad bowl.

Core and slice the apples and toss in half the lemon juice, then mix with the artichoke hearts, chopped celery, pecan nuts and grapes.

Blend the mayonnaise with the remaining lemon juice and the lemon zest, then add to the artichoke heart mixture and mix lightly.

Pile the mixture in the centre of the lettuce leaves, garnish with celery leaves and serve.

Serves **4 to 6**
Preparation time **10 minutes**

450 g/1 lb tinned artichoke hearts
1 Romaine lettuce, roughly shredded
2 green dessert apples
4 Tbsp lemon juice
4 celery sticks, chopped
50 g/2 oz pecan nuts
75 g/3 oz white seedless grapes
6 Tbsp mayonnaise
1 Tbsp grated lemon zest

TO GARNISH
Chopped celery leaves

SPICY PEPPER & MUSHROOM SALAD

THIS COLOURFUL AND APPEALING SALAD IS IDEAL TO SERVE WITH MANY OF THE FONDUES: TRY IT WITH THE BEEF, POULTRY OR FISH RECIPES.

Serves **4**

Preparation time

15 minutes

Cooking time **10 minutes**

1 red pepper

1 green pepper

1 yellow pepper

225 g/8 oz button
    mushrooms

8 spring onions, trimmed
    and chopped

3 Tbsp black olives, stoned
    and roughly chopped

Salad leaves

DRESSING

½ tsp crushed dried chillies

1 garlic clove, crushed

Salt and freshly ground black
    pepper

4 Tbsp olive oil

1 to 2 tsp clear honey

1 Tbsp balsamic vinegar

TO SERVE

Freshly grated Parmesan
    cheese and basil sprigs

Cut the peppers into quarters and remove the seeds and membrane. Line the grill rack with aluminium foil, arrange the peppers on the foil and place under a preheated grill for 10 minutes or until the skins have charred. Remove the peppers, place in a plastic bag and leave for about 10 minutes or until cool enough to handle. Skin and slice thinly, and place in a bowl.

Wipe and thinly slice the mushrooms, and add to the peppers with the spring onions and olives.

Place all the ingredients for the dressing in a screwtop jar and shake vigorously until blended. Pour over the peppers and mushrooms and toss lightly.

Arrange the salad leaves on a serving plate and top with the pepper and mushroom mixture. Sprinkle with the Parmesan cheese and basil sprigs to serve.

CREAMY POTATO & APPLE SALAD

THIS SALAD IS DELICIOUS SERVED WARM OR COLD.

Serves **4**

Preparation time

10 minutes

Cooking time

15 minutes

450 g/1 lb new potatoes

1 medium onion, chopped

6 spring onions, trimmed and chopped

4 celery sticks, trimmed and chopped

2 dessert apples

2 Tbsp lemon juice

50 g/2 oz pecan nuts

4 to 6 Tbsp mayonnaise

2 Tbsp natural or Greek yoghurt

Salt and freshly ground black pepper

Lettuce leaves

2 Tbsp chopped fresh mint

Scrub the potatoes, cut in half and cook in lightly salted boiling water for 15 minutes or until tender. Drain and, when cool, dice.

Place the potatoes in a bowl and add the chopped onion, spring onions, and celery.

Peel the apples if preferred, then core and dice them, and toss in the lemon juice to keep them from going brown. Stir into the potato mixture with the pecan nuts.

Blend the mayonnaise with the yoghurt and seasoning, add to the potato mixture and stir until lightly coated. Turn into a lettuce-lined salad bowl, sprinkle with the mint and serve.

MINT & LEMON TABBOULEH

THIS DELICIOUS SALAD COULD BE SERVED AS AN STARTER AS WELL AS AN ACCOMPANYING SALAD.

Serves **6 to 8**
Preparation time
   12 minutes plus 10 minutes standing time

225 g/8 oz bulgur wheat
4 medium tomatoes
½ small cucumber, peeled and diced
8 spring onions, trimmed and chopped
75 g/3 oz raisins
2 Tbsp chopped fresh parsley
2 Tbsp chopped fresh mint
2 Tbsp grated lemon zest
2 Tbsp lemon juice
4 Tbsp olive oil
Salt and freshly ground black pepper

Cover the bulgur wheat with tepid water and leave for about 10 minutes, stirring occasionally. Line a colander with a clean dish towel and drain the bulgur wheat, pressing out as much water as possible. Stir with a fork to separate the grains and place in a bowl.

Cut the tomatoes into quarters, deseed if preferred and chop finely. Add the tomatoes and cucumber to the bulgur wheat.

Stir in the spring onions, raisins, chopped herbs and lemon zest, and mix lightly.

Blend the lemon juice and olive oil, season, then pour over the salad. Mix lightly before serving.

RED BEAN & PEPPERONI SALAD

THIS SALAD IS ALMOST A MEAL IN ITSELF. IF YOU ARE CATERING FOR BOTH VEGETARIANS AND MEAT-EATERS, SERVE THE PEPPERONI SEPARATELY.

Serves **4**
Preparation time
   8 to 10 minutes

400 g/14 oz tinned red kidney beans
3 shallots, finely sliced
1 red serrano chilli, deseeded and chopped
100 g/4 oz cherry tomatoes, halved
6 spring onions, trimmed and chopped
75 g/6 oz pepperoni, sliced then diced
1 Tbsp chopped fresh parsley
1 Tbsp snipped fresh chives
1 to 2 tsp Worcestershire sauce
3 Tbsp olive oil
1 Tbsp red wine vinegar
Salt and freshly ground black pepper

Drain the kidney beans and rinse under cold water before placing in a bowl with the shallots and chilli. Add the tomatoes, spring onions, pepperoni and chopped herbs.

Blend the Worcestershire sauce with the oil and vinegar, and season to taste. Pour over the salad and toss lightly. Place in a serving bowl and serve.

DESSERTS

WHITE CHOCOLATE & TOFFEE SWIRL
FONDUE

WHEN BUYING CHOCOLATE FOR COOKING, LOOK FOR THE BEST AVAILABLE. THE HIGHER THE COCOA BUTTER CONTENT, THE BETTER THE FLAVOUR.

Break the chocolate into small pieces and place in the fondue pot with the double cream.

Place over a moderate heat and cook gently, stirring frequently until the chocolate has melted and is smooth and creamy. Carefully transfer to the lighted spirit stove.

Place the sugar, golden syrup and butter in a small pan and heat gently until blended. Remove from the heat and stir in the single cream.

Carefully swirl the toffee sauce on top of the white chocolate fondue, then serve with the fresh fruit and sweet biscuits for dipping.

Serves **6 to 8**
Preparation time **5 minutes**
Cooking time **6 to 8 minutes**

225 g/8 oz white chocolate
150 ml/$\frac{1}{4}$ pt double cream
2 Tbsp demerara sugar
1 Tbsp golden syrup
2 Tbsp butter
2 Tbsp single cream

TO SERVE
Pear and pineapple wedges, strawberries, hazelnut spongecake and Italian biscotti biscuits for dipping

LUSCIOUS VELVETY CHOCOLATE
FONDUE

THIS FONDUE IS DEFINITELY NOT FOR THE FAINT-HEARTED. IT'S RICH AND DECADENT—
ABSOLUTELY HEAVEN ON EARTH. AS WITH ALL DESSERT FONDUES, THIS CAN BE PREPARED
IN THE POT AND SERVED WITHOUT PLACING OVER A LIGHTED SPIRIT STOVE: THIS WILL MAKE
THE FONDUE EVEN MORE LUSCIOUS AND WICKED, AS IT THICKENS UP ON COOLING, GIVING
YOU MORE CHOCOLATE WITH EACH DIP.

Break the chocolate into small pieces, place in the fondue pot and
pour in the cream, rum or Cointreau and sugar if using.

Place over a moderate heat and cook, stirring frequently until melted
and thoroughly blended.

Carefully transfer the fondue pot to the lighted spirit stove and serve
with the amaretti biscuits, chocolate chip cookies, strawberries and
banana pieces, speared on to the fondue forks as dippers.

Serves **6 to 8**
Preparation time **5 minutes**
Cooking time **6 minutes**

225 g/8 oz plain dark chocolate
250 ml/8 fl oz double cream
3 to 4 Tbsp rum or Cointreau
1 Tbsp granulated brown sugar,
   optional

TO SERVE
Amaretti biscuits, chocolate chip
   cookies, strawberries and
   banana pieces for dipping

NUTTY MILK CHOCOLATE FONDUE

WHEN YOU ARE GOING TO SERVE A DESSERT FONDUE IT IS ESSENTIAL TO PLAN ANY STARTER AND THE MAIN COURSE CAREFULLY. AS THE DESSERT WILL BE VERY RICH, YOU NEED TO SERVE LIGHTER COURSES BEFOREHAND.

Serves **4**
Preparation time **4 to 5 minutes**
Cooking time **6 to 8 minutes**

225 g/8 oz milk chocolate
1 to 2 Tbsp maple syrup
150 ml/¼ pt double cream
2 Tbsp rum
75 g/3 oz toasted hazelnuts, roughly
  chopped

TO SERVE
Apple wedges and orange
  segments (allow one
  whole fruit per person),
  tiny meringues, and
  brandy snaps for dipping

Break the chocolate into small pieces and place in the fondue pot with the maple syrup, cream and rum.

Heat gently, stirring frequently until the chocolate has melted and is smooth and creamy.

Stir in the hazelnuts and serve with the pieces of fruit, meringues and brandy snaps for dipping.

MAPLE & CINNAMON FONDUE

BOTH FRIENDS AND FAMILY WILL BE BOWLED OVER BY THIS DECADENT AND DELICIOUS FONDUE. IT IS SO GOOD YOU WILL BE LICKING YOUR LIPS FOR HOURS!

Serves **4**
Preparation time **3 to 4 minutes**
Cooking time **5 minutes**

50 g/2 oz butter
175 g/6 oz granulated brown sugar
1½ tsp ground cinnamon
350 ml/12 fl oz single cream
2 Tbsp maple syrup
2 Tbsp cornflour

TO SERVE
Strawberries, melon balls,
  pineapple and mango
  wedges, sponge fingers
  and digestive biscuits
  for dipping

Place the butter with the sugar and a teaspoon of the ground cinnamon in a saucepan and heat gently until the sugar has dissolved. Stir well. Bring to the boil and cook for 1 minute.

Stir the cream and syrup into the pan. Blend the cornflour with the tablespoon of water and stir into the pan. Cook, stirring until the mixture thickens.

Pour into the fondue pot and carefully place over the lighted spirit stove. (If the fondue is overheated it will burn slightly—if this starts to happen, remove from the heat for a short time.) Sprinkle with the remaining cinnamon. Serve with the fruit and biscuits for dipping.

BRANDIED ORANGE
FONDUE

FOR THIS FONDUE IT IS WORTH USING FRESHLY SQUEEZED ORANGE JUICE RATHER THAN FROZEN CONCENTRATE. IT IMPROVES THE FLAVOUR AND YOU HAVE THE ADDED BONUS OF ATTRACTIVE FLECKS OF ORANGE IN THE FINISHED FONDUE.

Serves **4**
Preparation time **3 minutes**
Cooking time **6 to 8 minutes**

225 g/8 oz plain dark chocolate
120 ml/3 fl oz freshly squeezed
   orange juice
4 Tbsp double cream
2 Tbsp brandy
1 tsp grated orange zest

TO SERVE
Profiteroles, ginger
   biscuits, chocolate mints
   and marshmallows for
   dipping

Break the chocolate into small pieces and place in the fondue pan with the orange juice. Heat slowly until the chocolate has melted, then stir until smooth.

Stir in the cream and heat gently. Stir the brandy into the fondue with the grated orange zest. Heat, stirring, until the mixture is smooth and creamy.

Place over the lighted spirit stove and serve with profiteroles, ginger biscuits, chocolate mints and marshmallows for dipping.

BLACKCURRANT CREAM
FONDUE

IF YOU USE SWEETENED BLACKCURRANT JUICE, OMIT THE SUGAR FROM THE RECIPE. HOWEVER, IF USING FRESH BLACKCURRANTS, POACH THEM GENTLY WITH WATER AND SUGAR TO TASTE, THEN BLEND IN A FOOD PROCESSOR TO FORM A SMOOTH PURÉE.

Serves **4**
Preparation time **3 to 4 minutes**
Cooking time **5 to 7 minutes**

475 ml/16 fl oz blackcurrant juice or
   purée
1 to 2 Tbsp lemon juice
2 to 3 Tbsp caster sugar, or to taste
250 ml/8 fl oz double cream
2 Tbsp port or Madeira
1½ Tbsp cornflour

TO SERVE
Banana pieces, strawberries,
   seedless grapes, pineapple
   wedges, macaroons and
   baby meringues for dipping

Pour all but 2 tablespoons of the blackcurrant juice or purée into the fondue pot and stir in the lemon juice and sugar to taste.

Place over a very low heat and heat gently until warm. Stir in the cream and port or Madeira.

Blend the cornflour with the reserved blackcurrant juice or purée, then stir into the fondue pot. Cook, stirring until the juice thickens. Carefully place over the lighted spirit stove.

Serve with the fruit, macaroons and meringues for dipping.

CREAMY MALLOW FONDUE

FOR THIS FONDUE I HAVE USED MIXED SUMMER BERRIES, BUT IT WORKS EQUALLY WELL
WITH JUST RASPBERRIES OR A MIXTURE OF STRAWBERRIES AND RASPBERRIES. AS WITH ALL
SWEET FONDUES, DUE TO THEIR HIGH SUGAR CONTENT, THERE IS A TENDENCY FOR THE
FONDUE TO BURN SLIGHTLY. IF THIS HAPPENS REMOVE FROM THE HEAT AND ALLOW TO
COOL; YOU CAN STILL DIP THE FRUITS AND COOKIES IN.

In a food processor blend the berries to a purée, then pour into the
fondue pot. Add the marshmallows and cream.

Place over a very low heat and cook gently, stirring frequently until
smooth. Take care that the mixture does not boil. Stir in the lemon
juice, then carefully transfer to the lighted spirit stove and serve with
the marshmallows, sponge fingers, macaroons and apple wedges
for dipping.

Serves **4**
Preparation time **3 to 4 minutes**
Cooking time **10 minutes**

225 g/8 oz mixed summer
   berries, thawed if frozen
225 g/8 oz marshmallows
150 ml/¼ pt double cream
1 to 2 Tbsp lemon juice

TO SERVE
Marshmallows, sponge fingers,
   macaroons and apple wedges
   for dipping

DARK CHERRY FONDUE

BUY CANNED STONED CHERRIES AS THIS WILL SAVE A LOT OF TIME. IF YOU WISH TO USE FRESH CHERRIES YOU WILL NEED TO POACH THEM GENTLY IN A SUGAR SYRUP FOR 10 TO 15 MINUTES FIRST.

Roughly chop the cherries. Stir 250 ml/8 fl oz of the cherry juice into the cream. Pour into the fondue pot, stir in the sugar and place over a gentle heat. Bring to a gentle boil, then stir in the cherries and kirsch.

Blend the arrowroot with 1 tablespoon of either cherry juice or water, then stir into the fondue pot and cook, stirring until the fondue thickens.

Carefully place over the lighted spirit stove and serve with the meringue fingers, marshmallows, fruit, coconut and shortbread fingers for dipping.

Serves **4**
Preparation time **5 to 8 minutes**
Cooking time **8 minutes**

425 g/14 oz tinned stoned black cherries, juice reserved
150 ml/¼ pt double cream
1 Tbsp caster sugar
1 Tbsp kirsch
1 Tbsp arrowroot

TO SERVE
Meringue fingers, marshmallows, pineapple wedges, melon balls, cubes of fresh coconut and shortbread fingers for dipping

INDEX